Divorce Your Story

A woman's guide to heal & live a thriving life after divorce

Tonya Carter

BEFORE YOU BEGIN!!

I have a FREE checklist to help you as you read this book. This checklist includes 20 additional tips that will help you divorce your story once and for all!

Visit https://www.divorceyourstorybook.com/freechecklist to get a copy!

Divorce Your Story

A woman's guide to heal & live a thriving life after divorce

Copyright © 2019 by Tonya Carter

ISBN: 978-1-7334248-0-6 (Paperback)

Editing by: Darnise Harper & Erica Anderson

Book Design by Chris Mahan

Printed in the United States of America

First printing edition 2019.

Tonya Carter
Atlanta, Ga
www.tonyacarter.com

Dedication

To my children Keyvaun & Kyla: I love you and there's nothing in the world that's impossible for you.

To my parents Larry & Betty Carter: I love you and thank you for your support and I thank God for parents like you.

To my dearest friends Dr. Clotovis Barker & Ebony Gaston, thank you both for your friendship! I couldn't ask for better sisters.

Testimonials

"When I first started, I was blaming myself and feeling guilty that I could've possibly fought harder and worked harder to keep my family together. I wasn't thinking about myself! I've always put the needs and wants of others ahead of mine. As a result I'd become emotionally unhealthy and when I no longer could suppress those emotions, I exploded. I am not afraid to say no to anything or anyone that will not allow me to be my best emotional self for me and my kids. I am now okay with tapping into how this played a part in the issues in my marriage. On the other hand, I accept that the part my ex played, I can't control and will possibly never get the answer or apology. I have to be okay with letting go of not having all the answers and just use the new tools that I have to know better and do better for myself and possibly in a new relationship if I get into one." ~ *Renee Jackson*

"I've come to have peace about my part, their part, and the truth. I have accepted what was, embraced what is and looking forward to what is coming. This challenge was confirmation for me that I am always on a road of recovery, exploration of this new normal and self-love and care. Also, no more stopping and starting those things that I know I need to be doing in all areas of my life. I am more than a conqueror and those things in my life are designed for me to have dominion over it, not the other way around!!" ~ *Janice Moss*

"I have learned so much about myself. I was so broken and bitter. I feel better emotionally and spiritually. This is just the beginning to feel comfortable in my own skin. Not looking for someone else to make me happy. Forgiving people who may never apologize and knowing it's ok. Being alone is not a bad thing anymore. Moving forward, onward and upward. The best part was drawing closer to my God as a whole person. Thank you Tonya for this amazing avenue for growth. You ROCK!!! I really appreciate this opportunity to begin my healing. The information on self-reflection and inner work was awesome. It's a must for all dealing with divorce." ~*Joy Dozier*

Table of Contents

INTRODUCTION

Divorce is a word that no one likes to be affiliated with due to the shame and guilt that goes along with it. Feelings of hurt, anger, unforgiveness and rejection set in because this wasn't part of the plan. The plan was to stay together. This causes you to question yourself and even your future. You feel alone because people around you don't understand. You may not receive support from others and possibly even experience a distance in communication with them. You may receive advice to "get over it" as if this person wasn't once a huge part of your life or you may be told, "There's someone else out here." which isn't what you need to hear in the moment of your grief. You're left questioning your self-identity as a woman, causing you to feel uncertain about who you are. Your emotions are high. You're mentally and physically drained. Your kids see their parents no longer together which could cause them to lash out and now you're left to rebuild a new life.

We all have our rock bottom and this is yours right now. When you're in this place, you feel hopeless. You're left to pick up the pieces and unaware on how to do so. You don't think you have the strength to push forward and being positive is just something you may not be able to do right now. What I've learned in the thirty eight years of my life is that anything we go through isn't who we are but an influence on how it shapes you. For a long time, I believed my divorce was who I was instead of viewing it as my experience. This false belief caused me to think I was a failure, I wasn't enough and I had to settle. When you hear the word divorce, it involves a marriage that didn't work out between two individuals. Even though this is true, I had to bring a different perspective to the word divorce. When I looked up the definition of the word divorce, its synonyms are: disassociate, detach, and disconnect.

Even though I was no longer with this person legally, I was still attached, associated and connected to the experience that because the marriage didn't work...I failed. When you stay connected to what happened, you remain stuck in a chapter that has closed. That was me! I was that woman who divorced the person, but stayed married to the story. The story of associating divorce with disappointment. The story of believing I was limited to how far I could go because I'm a single mom. The story of believing that I couldn't rewrite a new chapter which resulted in allowing life to write it for me. Staying trapped in your story doesn't give you the ability to change the narrative. Instead of just leaving the situation, you must divorce it all, create a new chapter and gain full custody of your life. I wish I could tell you that just because you're divorced, that everything is going to work out on its own, however it takes more than just leaving the relationship. You must get through the experience. The understanding of disconnecting yourself from anything, anyone and any emotion that could hinder your ability to thrive. If you don't divorce the experience, it will show up in all areas of your life from your relationship with others to even the one you've established with yourself. You will always use your experience as the excuse and not the reason to execute. I encourage you that as you read this book, to have an open mind and to see things in a different light. I couldn't go in with the mindset of what I was conditioned to because the mindset that I initially had didn't work. I had to shift and be open to different information that was going to help me move forward and thrive. This book isn't about surviving.

Survivors have a "fixed" mindset and can barely keep their head above water. They allow themselves to be in total isolation to figure it all out of their own. They also allow themselves to settle and be a victim of their circumstances. However, your goal is to thrive. You don't want to just keep your head above water, but you want to swim. You want to put yourself in a position where you don't let your divorce defeat you. Your divorce isn't who you are, it's only what you've experienced. The question is: How are you going to allow this experience to shape you? When are you going to pick up the pen and start a new chapter?

Always remember, you are the author and you control what's being written.

Oh, and by the way, grab yourself a journal because there is an assignment for you after every chapter!

Chapter 1

Divorce Your Past

My marriage was over and I knew it too. I knew deep down that there was no possibility of it working out anymore. I was emotionally and mentally done. We became more like roommates than teammates and there was nothing else that could be done to reconcile.

Even though I knew that this was the best decision, it didn't mean that it was easier to do. Let's be honest, who really gets married to get a divorce? Who truly signs up for that? Nobody. But I also had to ask myself: Why would I stay? Was it because we had children? Was it because from the outside it "looked" good to stay together? Was it because I didn't want to feel like I was a failure? Was it because I wanted to make my parents proud? Was it because I made a covenant that I didn't want to break? All those reasons seemed like valid reasons to stay, but in reality they weren't. I didn't have a deeper why on why we needed to stay together anymore. It was time for us to move on.

You could be reading this right now and thinking, "YES! That's what I want to do! I want to move on!" but you may be wondering "How?"

For some, they believe that once they walk away from this person and once papers are signed, their life is just going to automatically be better and it's all going to work itself out by default. I'm not going to disagree and say that walking away wasn't the best option for you because chances are it may have been, but it doesn't just stop there. Getting a divorce alone is not going to be the solution. It's how you move forward from the divorce that's going to determine the outcome. I really thought that once I walked away from this marriage and signed papers that everything was just going to work out. That is until I woke up four and a half years later after my divorce and realized that my life was exactly the same. It hadn't really changed much. Only that I was a different age, it was a different year, but it was the same exact thing.

I had lost five jobs in four years which created a

"settling" mindset in the marketplace. I kept dealing with the same type of relationships from men. I even settled on opportunities because I used being divorced and being a single mom as the excuse for many things. I actually thought that those were valid reasons, but all that did was put a ceiling on how far I could climb. It made me settle for things that I never truly wanted. It made me miss out on opportunities that I never gave myself the ability to go after. I allowed being divorce to shape me as a person who felt limited and stuck to what life could offer me. Many wonder why they still feel stuck even after something that didn't work, which is why going through this is only a part of the solution. The rest of the solution is saying, "Am I going to stay stuck in it or am I going to grow from it?"

"The only thing worse than being blind is having sight but no vision" ~ *Helen Keller*

At only 19 months old, Helen Keller was faced with two disabilities. She became blind and deaf. However, she didn't allow those disabilities to disable her. She allowed those disabilities to push her. She learned many levels on how to communicate such as touch-lip reading, Braille, speech, typing and finger-spelling. She obtained a bachelor's degree. She traveled around the world as an activist to share her story to help others in the blind and deaf community as well as becoming an author. Helen could've used being blind and deaf as her excuse and many would have agreed that her reasons were valid but her condition wasn't who she was, it was just an experience that she had in life. I want you to be more like Helen Keller. Start looking beyond what your physical eyes can see because right now what you see may not be what it is you had planned in your mind. You got a divorce. You could be a single mom right now. You may not like that your finances are not where they need to be. You feel like you've invested everything into this relationship and the return you wanted never yielded. Let's admit, these are the types of things that could make you angry, develop resentment, and maybe even some bitterness right now. Let's think beyond the current and start thinking about our future self. What would you want your future self to look like? In other words, what do you want?

When you often ask people what do they want, you get surface responses like: "I want to be happy" or "I want a better life" but what does that mean? We have to paint that picture on what that new life looks like. We have to get more intentional and detailed about what it is we truly want. What I found out in myself was that I kept repeating the same chapters in the book of my life because I wasn't intentional. I didn't set a vision because I thought getting a divorce was the solution to all my issues.

If right now you're hurting and you have an emotional wound, what do you want from that? How would you like to heal? If you feel like your relationship with your kids will be impacted because of the divorce, how can you make sure that relationship is stronger than ever? If you believe that where you are professionally isn't enough, then what would you like to see happen in your professional life? And most importantly, how would you want the relationship to be with yourself? You may feel like you can't identify that woman in the mirror anymore. That woman is hurt, broken, angry, ashamed and could feel like a total failure right now. What would you like to see come from all of this? How can you take what you view as pain to push you? Starting over sometimes can be hard because it seems like you're starting from ground zero, but sometimes in life you have to break down to rebuild in order to form a new & improve masterpiece. When you see torn buildings being rebuilt and getting remodeled, it's being remodeled for improvement which is what you're doing with yourself. Think of yourself as being in the rebuilding phase and allowing that vision that you're working towards to be your masterpiece.

Have you ever noticed how many people put so

much effort into someone else's vision that they don't attempt to place an effort in theirs? Was that you? Did you place so much effort in the relationship that you forgot the effort you needed to place in yourself as well? Do you make everyone else's needs matter where you never allowed yourself to take care of your own needs? Did you know that you are a personal brand? Chances are you may have never looked at it that way, but it's time you start. How can you live a better life when you don't have anything to look forward to? This is why you need vision. You need direction on where you need to go to be who you want to become. Don't let this experience cause you to lose sight of what's ahead for you because in order for you to move on from this, you are going to have to divorce your past and marry your new vision.

What do you want your life to look like from this point forward? What do you envision yourself to be? What do you want to have? Be clear and specific on what it is that you want because the clearer you are with what you want, the more of an aim you have.

Thrive it out!

In your journal, write out your vision statement.

- Think about how you want to heal

      o Who do you want to become?

      o Think of the fundamental areas of your life that make you whole to help with your vision statement (i.e. Spiritually, Mentally, Emotionally, Financially, Professionally etc.)

Chapter 2

Divorce the Fear

Moving forward requires you to actually *move*. That means in order to take action, you have to move your feet. Writing down your vision statement was just a part of it, but it's the daily activity that's going to get you towards your vision. Sometimes we fear moving forward because we honestly don't know what the road ahead looks like. Even though you know staying where you are doesn't make sense, it's still your normalcy. It's that uncomfortable comfort zone that you know all too well. I was so used to an unhealthy life and because of that, I didn't have any certainty of what the future consisted of. I realized that I became content with the life I already had because I knew what I was getting myself into. I once believed that some people didn't have fear and other people did. But developing fearlessness isn't an "either you have it or you don't" ability, it's about doing it in spite of what's unfamiliar. In other words, you must move regardless of how much it scares you.

When my marriage ended, I felt like a loser. I was that type of individual who always strived to win at everything that I committed myself to. When it didn't work out as planned, it planted a fear of not being good enough, causing me to be stuck in my story and not moving forward. This was all I knew. I invested so much in it. Because I was unfamiliar with what was coming, I decided to stay stagnant. As long as I viewed myself as a failure, I could never allow myself to develop fearlessness in me. I had to change the way I viewed my experience. My experience used to say, "You're a failure," but for me to move forward it said "You're not a failure, it just didn't work out." These are two totally different ways to view this. There were a lot of things in my life that didn't work out as planned. However, I turned out to be okay, and so will you. I had to get out of the mindset of failure because that wasn't going to allow me to get to my vision. I had to learn that in life you either win or you learn, the only time a person fails is when they give up on themselves.

You could be in a place of fear right now. You may fear not being good enough. You may fear that you could end up lonely. You may even fear making decisions because of the past decisions you have made but ask yourself these questions: What are you gaining by staying where you are? What are you losing by not moving?

Earlier this year, I had a young lady by the name of Lisa who started my *21 Day Divorce Detox Program* to help get through her divorce. She told me that she just couldn't do it. I asked her why. She said she just wasn't ready, even though she knew it was time to move forward. Lisa mentioned that she just wasn't ready to move. She felt stuck and didn't know how to get unstuck even though she was getting the tools that was needed to move forward. Lisa chose to stay stuck because of fear. Sometimes we believe that we're just going to wake up and fear is going to be thrown out the window and we're going to all of a sudden become fearless. I wish I could tell you that this was true but that's not how it works. You minimize the doubt by doing it in spite of how you feel. I remember being that woman who chose to stay stuck even though I didn't verbally say it, but my actions proved otherwise. This was one of my biggest regrets. What I realized was that I was stuck in my story for almost five years. That was 60 months, 260 weeks, 1,825 days, & 43,800 hours, which is time I can NEVER get back. If you want to know the truth, there will NEVER be a perfect time! The perfect time is the time you have and that is now. You don't want to be that individual who looks up a year from now and you're in the exact same place if not worse because you didn't do the most important thing and that is to heal.

Allow your "Why" to push you!

My kids mean everything to me. I gave them everything I could possibly give them. I put them in every activity I could, spent lots of time with them, bought them things they wanted, showed up to all school functions, kept them up to date on all doctor appointments, a roof over their heads, etc. I pretty much did what seemed to be what a parent should do, but without an emotionally healthy mom, what would that do to them? How would that make an impact on their relationship with others? Most importantly, how would that play an impact on the relationship they developed within themselves? This was more about the future consequences. It was time to look beyond where I was and think about the future I wanted to see produced. I had to think less about my fear and more about who would benefit from me moving forward. I realized that moving forward wasn't about me. It was about something bigger. One thing I learned about life is that something has to be able to push you into becoming a fearless individual. My kids were my fuel to turn that fear into faith. Instead of coming up with reasons as to why moving forward wasn't possible, it was time to understand why this was necessary.

I want you to take a look at your vision statement that you wrote and if you hadn't written down your vision statement, please go back and do so because it's important that you go beyond your current self and see who needs you to heal. Who's counting on you? Is it your children? Is it somebody else who might be going through it later on and they need your story to get through? I want you to think much bigger than just yourself. Who needs you?

Thrive it out!

In your journal, write out the people who need you

-Think about who will benefit from your healing & what will the benefit be

-Think about the long term consequences of staying in a fearful place

- For every fearful belief you have, replace it with a fearless belief

Tonya Carter

Chapter 3

Divorce Your Vocabulary

Have you ever caught yourself saying, "I knew this was going to happen!"or "I said that this was going to happen!" and you sit there and you wonder, "Why did this happen?" Yep! I did the exact same thing. I used to always speak what I didn't want into existence. According to Merriam-Webster, there isn't an exact count of the number of words in English because the English language is always expanding. This tells you that for every word that you don't want to use, there's always a better word that can be used. When I was in high school and before I took my SAT's, I took a class to help me expand my vocabulary. Doing this allowed me to be more creative with the words that I used and also to gain insight on the different words that can be used. There were so many words that I was unfamiliar with. There was always another word I could use to substitute another word with even though it had the exact same meaning. There were also words that I could use to replace what I didn't want to say. I came to the understanding that before I was studying for the SAT, I was limited in the number of words in my vocabulary.

Oftentimes, we're not really speaking life over our situation. We're actually speaking words of death. The words "I can't", "This could never happen to me", "This is impossible", and "I'm a total failure" are not words that produce life.

There's a quote by Maya Angelou that says:

"People will forget what you said, people will forget what you did, but people will never forget how you made them feel."

During my marriage, hurtful words were exchanged between me and my spouse. Do I remember everything that my spouse and I said to one another? I don't. What I do remember is how those words made me feel. As I look back and reflect, there were many other vocabulary words that I could've used from Merriam-Webster. I could've used words that didn't hurt but instead words of help and love. Your words are powerful! They can either build you up or tear you down. Not only did I say hurtful words in my marriage,

I also said hurtful words to myself. If I didn't like hurtful words being said to me from other people, why would I say hurtful words to myself?

When I saw how my life was playing out, it made me see that my reality came from my vocabulary. My story was "This couldn't happen to me", and guess what? It didn't happen. My story was "This was impossible", and guess what? It was, and it wasn't because it was actually true, it was because I believed it to be true. I entertained and attracted what I didn't want because I didn't believe anything else could come. It didn't matter what I wrote down or what I said. If I wasn't developing a new "believe" system over my life, then how could I expect anything new to come into fruition?

Your "believe" system

Your "believe" system is what your mind is filled with. They are thoughts that you have on a daily basis that determine how you move. They are also feelings that you have about life, others, as well as yourself. Our thoughts can be formed by everything from our upbringing, to the things that have been said to us and even past life circumstances. My words were a reflection of my thoughts. Anything that came from my mouth was from what I believed. I never knew I had control over my thoughts. My philosophy was, this was how

I thought and there was nothing I could do about it. In other words, I didn't know that I had the power to change my way of believing. I had a stationary mindset which hindered my ability to believe anything more than my current thoughts.

When I made a decision to divorce my story, I had to divorce my way of thinking. How could I get to my vision with the same mindset that got me here? That's not possible. To upgrade my life, my mind had to first be upgraded. It's no different than driving a car to where you want to go. If the car isn't working properly then how would you get to the destination? You can't. In order to get to your destination, the car must be in good working condition to get there. That's similar to how your mind works, because where your mind leads....you will follow.

Our mind produces 50,000 – 70,000 thoughts per day. Even though we can't remember them all, it's important to take into account the sum total of your thoughts. It's time to start thinking about what you're thinking about. I like to consider myself a well-organized individual. I do my best to keep things together at home and at work. I write things down and put things on my calendar so I can stay up-to-date and I don't get behind. I keep track of almost everything but I never kept track of my thoughts. That was one thing that I never allowed myself to take inventory of. When I started paying close attention to what I was thinking, I saw why my life was how it was. I believed all of it! I would want one thing, but I believed another. Your mind is just that powerful! In the words of Earl Nightingale, "You become what you think about".

Have you ever just took the time to take inventory of your thoughts? What are they? Are they more positive or negative? Are they thoughts of life or death? No matter what they are, they can always be the thoughts you want them to be. Think of your mind as a garden, if what you've been planting in your mind isn't what you want to be produced, then plant something else. For instance, if you've been planting seeds of poison, then plant roses instead. Those roses are thoughts of what you want to see take place. Those roses are thoughts of how you want to view yourself. Those roses are thoughts of what will get you to your vision.

Is it easy? No! But it's simple. All it takes is a shift. First, show yourself some compassion for a change. If your close friend, family member or child came to you and told you that they were a failure, they couldn't do it and this wasn't possible, what would you say? We tend to give compassion to those we love but we forget the fact that we should love ourselves just as much to use those same words of power over ourselves.

Second, be more intentional with the words you speak. Start monitoring your words and pay close attention to your choice of words. If they're words that won't produce roses, catch what you say, replace it with what you want to see happen and repeat.

Third, take it a step further and look around you. Notice the conversations you have with others, the television shows you watch, the people you follow on social media to even the music you listen to. Are these things in alignment with your thoughts? Will it help you get to your vision? I didn't realize how much this had an impact on my life until I started becoming more self-aware of my environment. I couldn't digest a lot of things anymore because it didn't fit in the direction that I wanted to go.

Fourth, pick up a book. Listen to motivational videos. Make sticky notes with "I AM" statements and place them on your bathroom mirror. Read devotionals. Voice record your vision and listen it to it at night. Start a daily gratitude journal.

Remember: You have to immerse yourself into this. It's not just going to happen on its own. You have to marry you a new mind and new words in order to believe and speak differently.

Thrive it out!

In your journal over the next few days, take inventory of your thoughts:

-On a scale of 1-10 (10 being the highest)
  o What were the sum total of your thoughts?
    o Positive –
    o Negative –

-What were the triggers of those thoughts
  o Examples – A song? A conversation with someone, A place you went to, Something you've read or watched on television, social media, etc.

-If your overall thoughts were negative, what can be done to alleviate it?
  o Examples – Not listen to that specific song and listen to something else that will empower you, Unfollow certain people on social media or do a fast, etc.

Tonya Carter

Chapter 4

Divorce the Blame

Legally, I've been divorced for nine years, but I've been living my life intentionally for a little over half of those years. For the first half of my divorce experience, I thought I was moving forward but the only thing that was moving were the years and my age. When I finally woke up, I saw that my life was being lived off blame. I stayed stuck in my story mostly because I blamed everything and everyone else for my life. When my marriage didn't work out, I blamed him for it. Anything I could blame him for, I did! I blamed him for what he didn't do, what he could have done, what he should have done, and how my life would have been better if he only had done it. I also blamed life. Losing five jobs in a four year timeframe really took its toll on me mentally as well as financially. It was easy to blame the government and the recession on how my life and finances were. I found myself blaming other men. Even post-divorce, I didn't think I was the issue. I was vulnerable but I didn't know it at the time and that caused me to get attached to someone I cared for who I thought also cared for me. However, it was just another heartbreak and so I blamed him. There was a part of me that blamed my parents even though I never told them this. I know my parents meant well in my life, from my education and even me being married. At that time their influence was high on my list and because I was angry and hurt from how my life was turning out to be, it made sense at that time to blame them too. Even from a spiritual place, I blamed God. I wondered "Why would God do this to me?"

Having this mentality generates a victim's mindset. I know sometimes we don't want to believe that because we feel justified in having the "Why me?" mentality. When I looked up the definition of the word blame, it is an assigned responsibility for a fault or wrong. When you operate from a place of blame you don't get anything from that place. It's a cycle that you can find yourself stuck in because it's easy to do. The only thing you get from blame is a repeated story over time. When you blame everything and everyone and even yourself for your life, you don't move much which causes you to become stagnant and stuck in your story.

When I decided to take power and control over my life that also meant that I needed to take ownership of it. When I looked up the word ownership, it's the act, state or right of possessing something. When you operate from a place of ownership, you take pride in it. Think about it. When you own a home, business, or even a car, you establish a sense of pride because you worked for it and you cherish it, but anything that comes from a place of blame, you don't treasure it neither do you take pride in it. If anything, you have more shame or even worse, you feel like you can justify why blaming makes sense.

In order for us to divorce the story, we have to become victors over it. We have to do less blaming and more owning. You can't live your best life from a place of blame. You can only live your best life from a place of ownership. In order for you to get out of your story, you have to divorce the blame. When I tell clients to take ownership, sometimes they automatically go to a place of saying, "This wasn't my fault. I'm not the one to blame!" which is the wrong interpretation of what taking ownership means. Ownership is saying that no matter what has happened to you, no matter what life has thrown you, it's important for you to take responsibility for your life. Ownership doesn't mean that everything that occurred in your life is your fault because everything in life isn't your fault. There are many things that are beyond our control however, there are a lot of things we can control and we do that by taking full ownership. It's easy to say "I was betrayed and my life is messed up because of them." It's harder to say "Even though they didn't do right by me, it's still my responsibility to keep moving forward." This is oftentimes the challenge but when you stop blame shifting and start taking ownership for yourself, you will live a thriving life.

How do we take ownership? You welcome it in. Allow yourself to bring ownership into your life and embrace it. You may not like where you are at the moment. To be honest, it may suck right now. You could be thinking of all the things that have taken place in your relationship. I'm not going to sit up here and say that life right now seems to be working out in your favor. However, it will never work out in your favor if you continue to operate from a place of blame. Even if you're blaming yourself, that's not the solution either. Taking ownership of your life doesn't mean to blame yourself. That's no different than you blaming other people. Ownership gives you the fuel that you need to move forward. It gives you the ability to change your perspective on dealing with this situation. In chapter one, you wrote your vision statement for your life. Go back and read your vision statement and ask yourself, will taking ownership get you there or will placing blame get you there? What will it feel like if you took ownership as opposed to blaming everything and everyone for your life? What would becoming the victor do for you life instead of being the victim?

Thrive it out!

In your journal, write down everyone & everything you've been placing the blame on. Below that, write the following:

"In order to divorce my story, I understand that everyone and every situation that I've written above are not valid reasons to stay a victim. For me to live a thriving life, I must first take FULL responsibility of it all! I can't control anyone except myself so from this day forward, if I start blaming something or someone, I will instantly remind myself that I AM THE OWNER AT ALL TIMES and no one or nothing will drive my life but me. I understand that this is a new lifestyle that requires dedication, being intentional and remaining faithful to the journey. I OWE ME!

Keep this nearby. Take a screenshot on your phone, give it to some friends that you know will cheer you on, post it on your refrigerator, on your bathroom mirror, and/or your desk at work.....wherever it's visible!

Tonya Carter

Chapter 5

Divorce Your Emotions

Think about the last time that you were physically hurt. This may have been a fall where you scraped your knee or arm. You may have accidentally burned your hand over a stove or maybe something even more critical like a broken arm, wrist or ankle. However, a wound is a wound and in order for that wound to heal properly, you have to go through a certain healing & treatment process. This process could be the cleaning of the wound and/or applying ointments. For more serious accidents, it may involve going to the doctor for x-rays or even physical therapy. Depending on the wound and how deep it is, there is a certain method that must be applied in order for that wound to heal correctly. I want you to think of your divorce similar as a physical wound. Even though it may not be something that you physically see, it is something that you feel emotionally. Oftentimes we believe we can escape these emotions by pretending that everything is okay from the outside, but internally it's not because you're hurt. Your heart is broken right now and placing a Band-Aid over it is not the fix to your problem.

"Owning our story can be hard but not nearly as difficult as spending our lives running from it. Embracing our vulnerabilities is risky, not as nearly as dangerous as giving up on love and belonging and joy – the experiences that make us the most vulnerable. Only when we are brave enough to explore the darkness will we discover the infinite power of our light." ˜ Dr. Brene Brown

Dr. Brene Brown, a researcher and vulnerability expert describes the definition of vulnerability as "uncertainty, risk and emotional exposure. It's the birthplace of love, belonging, joy, courage, empathy and creativity. It is the source of hope, empathy, accountability and authenticity. If we want greater clarity in our purpose or deeper meaningful spiritual lives, vulnerability is the path, it is the core of all emotions and feelings".

When I read this in her book *"Daring Greatly"*, let's just say originally I didn't get that deep about vulnerability and the importance of it. When I thought of the word vulnerable, I automatically thought it meant weakness. Growing up I was never taught to express my emotions, let alone deal with them. I was taught to be strong but not in the sense of being vulnerable according to Dr. Brown's definition. Strong for me was to keep everything inside. It meant to not show emotion. It meant to get over things and act as if everything was normal. I was the type of individual that if you asked me how I was doing, I would just say that I'm okay. Deep down I always knew I wasn't, I just didn't allow myself to be vulnerable about how I felt. I didn't know how to take off the mask. However, if I really wanted to live the life that I wrote down in my vision statement, being the type of strong woman that I've always been wasn't going to get me there. I had to explore the darkness of my emotions and what I was dealing with internally and to do that, it required me to be vulnerable.

We've all experienced losing a loved one. Everybody comes over, from family, friends, and people that you may even work with. They console you, bring food, help you out around the house, and run errands for you. They may even give you money to help you out with expenses. You're told that you'll be okay and they make sure to let you know that you will get through this. They say "Call if you need anything" and they'll be there. Most importantly, they tell you to grieve. Your divorce is equivalent to losing a loved one. I know you may have family and friends that don't really get this. Some believe that because you're no longer together that you have no feelings about it. The support that many receive when losing a loved one might not be what you're getting right now. Sometimes you may lose friends and you're left to figure this all out. You could be thinking "Am I crazy?" or "Should I not be feeling this way?" Well, I'm here to tell you that you're not crazy and it's normal to feel this way. You must allow yourself permission to grieve this process. We think it's a badge of honor to always be okay and pretend as if nothing is going on, but it's okay to not be okay, it's just not okay to stay that way.

In order to divorce your story, you must fully own it and part of fully owning your story is to feel your emotions. It means that you must take the mask off and really allow yourself to feel what's hurting you. I can't lie, this was a scary place to go to, but doing it allowed me to be honest with myself for a change. I didn't care anymore about what everybody else thought and how anyone felt on where I should be. Being society's definition of strong was no longer important to me anymore. What was important was my healing because when I was operating from a place of hurt, it caused me to make permanent decisions based on temporary feelings such as emotional spending, hanging out drinking on the weekends, even dealing with unhealthy relationships. It caused me to numb my emotions so much that I didn't allow myself to face the reality of my situation at that time, not to mention blaming everything and everyone for my life, which kept me stuck in my story.

I want to pose a question to you: How are you doing emotionally? That's a much different question than just saying, how are you doing? Your default answer when someone asks you how you are doing, is probably, "I'm fine" or "I'm okay" or "I can't complain" because you don't want anyone to see or know how you're doing. I'm here to ask you how you are doing emotionally because your emotions are real at the moment. They are not permanent. They are temporary, but those are the feelings that you have at this present moment, they are real and you need to tap into them.

Many of us think we can escape our emotions, but you can never escape your emotions. The only way you can fully allow yourself to deal with your emotions is to welcome them in & don't ignore them. Acknowledge that this is how you feel and get curious about why. This will create self-awareness as well as an increase in your emotional intelligence. Oftentimes, we numb our emotions believing that as long as we don't deal with them, they will just vanish on their own, but they show up in your life in other ways because you're allowing yourself to escape the current reality when you need to allow yourself to confront what's in front of you. When you numb your emotions, you may substitute them for things like consumption of alcohol or becoming an emotional eater. Your calendar is so busy to keep your mind occupied that you don't deal with what's really bothering you. You can self-sabotage anything great that comes your way because you could be operating from a place of hurt. You may withdraw yourself from family and friends. You start living on autopilot and not looking towards what the future can bring, causing you to stay stuck. You can never be fully present in a relationship due to buried emotions. You may also become an emotional spender, creating debt that will be a challenge to pay off. You could attempt to seek revenge on your ex or stalk him. You may hate being by yourself so you're willing to be around anyone or anything no matter how unhealthy it is, just to have a sense of belonging. You may even find yourself having meaningless sex with multiple partners, living behind your children, and/or being in denial about your situation.

One of my emotions was guilt. I felt guilty because I broke a covenant, a promise that I made to God. That cut deep for me. I wasn't the type of individual to do that. My parents have been married for almost 50 years, and so the covenant and making a promise to stay together meant something to me. I felt guilty because I thought that I couldn't give my kids something that they needed and that was a family. I felt like I broke up my family. I felt like my divorce indicated that I wasn't a good wife and it made me believe that I was a complete and total failure. I also experienced a lot of anger. The anger came from many things. One was that I had invested all this time emotionally, physically and financially. This was the return that I was going to receive? A divorce? That isn't fair! The return wasn't supposed to be a divorce, it was to stay married...well at least that was what I thought. The anger I felt was from always being in a financial bind due to money being one of our main issues. I never felt secure in our marriage, even in the area of finances. Constantly spending our money irresponsibly left so much frustration, not to mention a lack of trust that I started to have towards him as a result of how he utilized our money. There were plenty of times when all I did was worry about whether or not the bills would get paid. When I was six months pregnant with our daughter, I had to go to work after we agreed that I would stay home until after our daughter was born. Here I am over halfway into my pregnancy and my focus was on finding a job to make sure bills were paid. Working was never an issue for me, but to deal with that when I only had three months left before our daughter was born could've been avoided. After our daughter was born, I remember my first night in the hospital my best friend stayed with me because he didn't. I thank God for her because I had a Cesarean and the pain of that was intense. I can't lie, I was so angry that my respect for him was slim to none. Now I will admit, we weren't on the best of terms but he was my husband and I wasn't just a random chick. Regardless of what we were going through, why not put that aside and be there in my time of need?

Seeing an email from him chatting with another woman really made me lose the little respect I had for him. When I called the woman and asked her how she knew my husband, she responded "I didn't even know he was married." Funny, I believed her. When I confronted him about it, there was no remorse about what he had done. Even though I stayed, I never looked at him the same. I remember when we were separated, shortly after he was already in another relationship. They started living together and ended up having a baby. I was not aware that he had a child until after the baby was born. How I found out and when I found out was devastating. I was at work and this was my last week at my job. I was getting laid off and I had so much going on. I texted him and when he texted me back, he mentioned that he had a child. Here I am at work trying to keep my composure because that was beyond what

I expected to get back in a text. By this time, we were separated a little over a year BUT he got her pregnant six months after we separated. My response to the text was "Congratulations" even though I didn't mean it at that time because I was really numb. When I left work, there wasn't a curse word that was eliminated from my vocabulary! I just couldn't receive that news very well. I was angry because he got married so quickly and I said to myself, "Wow! Did he even grieve our relationship?" As I reflect, I knew it bothered me more than I wanted it to, but here I was masking it. I wanted to cry and not hear the words "be strong." I wanted to know that it's okay to feel this way and not believe that I was wrong for those emotions. Everything was becoming too much. This was my third lay off, our divorce wasn't final, I was dealing with thoughts of fear and doubting whether I would be able to take care of my home and he already started another family. Yes, I had reached a full level of pissocity!

Anger was an emotion that I was attached to but dealing with it in a healthy way wasn't something I knew about. That anger led to depression, constantly going out on Saturday nights and dealing with other unhealthy relationships. Anger is something we all experience, but don't necessarily know how to process. All that anger I was experiencing was nothing but deep layers of hurt, sadness, and disappointment. I was hurt because of the lack of commitment I received from someone who was considered to be my husband. I was sad because his actions didn't show protection, security and love. I was disappointed because over the course of our marriage, I didn't feel like I ever received the respect I should've gotten.

People will tell you not to be angry, feel hurt or have any other emotion that makes them uncomfortable. This is not realistic if that's the emotion you feel. This led me to numb everything which only delayed my healing, not to I felt like I couldn't express what I was going through. I came to realize my anger was a valid emotion, it's just how we deal with it that determines the outcome. Your emotions could be on a roller coaster right now and people may tell you that you shouldn't feel this way and you may even ask yourself, "This relationship wasn't working, so why am I feeling this way?" That's what you call a normal emotion from a person who has lost someone who was once a part of their lives. Even though this is a normal experience to have, we cannot stay in this particular space.

Because divorce is in close relation to losing a loved one, there are five different stages of grief that was originally introduced by Psychiatrist Elisabeth Kubler-Ross to help with grief and loss. Most likely, you will find yourself fitting in these stages:

1. **Denial** – Not really dealing with the reality but instead living in a "preferable" reality. You could be having a difficult time digesting what is happening right now, regardless of who chose to walk away. You may experience feelings of avoidance, confusion, elation, shock and/or fear. Denial could also help you cope & survive with the initial event. Doing this allows you to pace your grief as opposed to be overwhelmed by it.

2. **Anger** – When reality starts to come in you may have thoughts of time invested, their actions, your actions as well as feelings of frustration, irritation and anxiety. You may believe that you shouldn't be angry when anger is an emotion that you shouldn't avoid but feel. You want to welcome it in with no intention of harming others or even yourself. Even though you may feel like the cycle is endless to your anger, it will diminish. The more its felt, the more it's reduced.

3. **Bargaining** – Going through this could cause you to want to undo any damage. You find yourself wanting to go back and may be willing to do anything to bargain, even in an unhealthy way rather than deal with the current pain. If you are the individual that didn't initiate the divorce, you could experience this stage more than the person who wanted to leave.

4. **Depression** – Depression can occur when we feel a sense of emptiness when realizing that the situation is really over. Decisions as well as adjustments from the divorce process can lead to a deep level of sadness. In this phase, you may

withdraw from friends & family, and you may not feel supported. You may also experience emotional numbness. Depression is normal and a part of your healing experience. What's abnormal is to not sense any response at all.

5. **Acceptance** – You're coming to a place of realizing that this is what it is. Your emotions start to become much calmer and you're beginning to understand that this isn't the end but instead an opportunity to create a new life. You may still experience moments of sadness but not like you used to. You've accepted that this is normal and will not be a determining factor on whether or not life goes on. At this point your good days will outweigh the bad days.

Over the next few weeks I want you to take inventory of your daily emotions. Your emotions may be up and down. One day you may feel great, the next day you may feel sadness. The next day you may feel guilt, shame, or a combination of emotions. The goal is to be in tune with those emotions and acknowledge the fact that this is how you feel in the present moment. However, having those emotions, it's important to know why you have that emotion. Write down the why behind the emotion. Ask yourself, "Why am I feeling this way?" and be completely and totally authentic. This can be written down in a journal, verbalized in a voice recorder, expressed with a trusted friend, a therapist and/or coach, but the goal is to be in tune with the emotion unapologetically.

Take Care of You!

When experiencing a divorce, we can fall off of things such as not taking care of ourselves like we would normally do. Make sure that you're getting enough sleep. Eat healthy foods. Get some exercise, but don't overdo it. Get your body moving to get those endorphins pumping because that lowers your stress levels and boosts your mood. Take a look at your vision statement and ask yourself, "Is my hurt going to get me there or will healing get me there?" Incorporate some things you love to do. What haven't you done in a while because of the divorce that you're experiencing? Self-care is essential to healing and doing things that make you smile can help you heal. Have you been to the movies or a comedy show? Have you invited your friends over just to watch a movie and just get a glass of wine and enjoy laughing? Laughing is known for boosting the mood to improve overall health. The support of your friends can help ease feelings of loneliness and isolation. I also recommend these four books to help you during this time:

1. *Rising Strong - Brene Brown*
2. *Daring Greatly - Brene Brown*
3. *The Gifts of Imperfection - Brene Brown (Clearly, I'm a*

fan of her work)
4. *You're a Badass - Jen Sincero*

Remember, during this process your emotions are yours and not of your ex. During this time of processing you could assume or believe that you can control how the ex is feeling but that's not your concern because the only person you can control is you.

If you feel that you're unable to do this, seek additional help. We often want to do everything on our own, and you may not be able to. Reach out for help, whether that be a therapist, a divorce coach such as myself, or if you have a community or church community go there and enroll in one of their programs (such as DivorceCare or Second Saturday) so you can be around other people that are going through the same experiences as you.

How long will I feel these emotions?

There's no magic formula or exact time frame on how long it's going to be. Every person and every situation is different. It's hard to determine how long it will take your heart to heal. However, I will say that the more intentional you are about your healing, the better your healing will be and the faster your healing will come. Every day when you wake up, you must be intentional about your healing. It has to be your #1 priority even on those days when you don't feel your best. Sometimes the journey of healing may seem uncertain. I wish I could tell you that every day you're going to feel great. You may not, but this doesn't mean that things aren't getting better. Your healing is similar to when you put money in the stock market, it compounds, which means that what you do daily will yield the results that you want.

You can be working on your healing for 30 days straight and not feel any different, but on day 31 you feel like a totally different person. This result came from the 30 days of effort that was put in prior to reaching day 31. Many prolong the healing because of being in denial, not even wanting to feel their emotions, or just the commitment of being on the journey of healing. Even though there's no exact timeframe, don't just give your healing time. Many say, "Just give it time, it will get better." Time alone will not heal you. It's time plus the daily action that will determine the intensity of healing.

Thrive it out!

In your journal, answer the following questions:

1. What stage(s) do you feel best describes you right now?
2. Why? (Be very transparent)
3. How long have you been in this stage(s)
4. What has been the result of being in this stage?
5. What forward approach can be taken to start detaching yourself from this stage? *If you're at a place of true acceptance how can you make sure you're constantly growing emotionally?*

Chapter 6

Divorce the Communication

"My ex wants to be friends." I've heard this so many times and I also found myself saying the same thing. If moving on is the goal, be careful and intentional when it comes to communicating with your ex. Can you all be "friends" right now? Or is this something that you're wanting to still be emotionally attached to? I don't want you to think that being enemies is what I'm hinting at because it's neither. It's about knowing where you are mentally and emotionally right now. In order for your healing to take place, you must keep the communication with the individual to a minimum.

Another part of not being together is understanding that you can't do the same things that you once did when you were married. Moving forward involves disconnecting yourself which also includes disconnecting the communication. In the beginning of our separation, I found myself still coming around to his family gatherings because this was all I knew. Those traditions were no longer a tradition of mine and accepting that this was no longer the case was challenging for me. I even found myself talking to him only to start an argument because I was operating from a place of hurt & I wanted him to feel my hurt. As much as I hate to admit it, I still wanted to be attached because this was all I knew. I didn't know anything else at that time but my unhealthy marriage. I even found myself asking him one time to go on vacation together. Even though we didn't go I did that because I still wanted to be connected to something that was already disconnected. Making the decision to move on doesn't just include signing papers. It doesn't just involve you not living together either. It also involves the type of communication that you have with this person. It's essential to create a gap, but not a gap of hating this person or even wanting this person to hurt, but just a healthy gap to realize that you need to heal and it's difficult to heal while continuing to be accessible like you're still married to them.

For some, they want to be friends, to stay connected, and to talk every day. You even have some people that still live together. You're following them on social media keeping up with everything they're doing. You're doing everything possible to still stay joined together even though you know being with them doesn't make sense. You're wondering why you're so emotionally confused and you don't know how to move forward. One of those reasons is due to the lack of change in communication. Maybe it's because of fear, loneliness, or you're hoping to get back together. You may be so accustomed to being a wife that you don't know how to divorce the benefits. For me this was a tough one, I was so used to helping him out that not helping felt strange. I was the accountant, the cook, the person who cleaned and took care of the household duties as well as worked outside the home. For many, you're working as the wife but you no longer have the benefits of one. When you're no longer at a job, the benefits stop. They no longer give you health or dental insurance. They don't continue to add to your 401K or give you vacation days. When the job is no longer available to you, the benefits are no longer available. Being a wife is an honor and it's a role that can emotionally confuse you if you allow yourself to still play a wifely role to someone that you're no longer a wife to. Even though that's a harsh reality, it's important to know that the benefits stop when there is no benefit of being with one another.

Well, what if we have children? This means that

you'll always have a relationship with this person, just a different type of relationship. It is critical to separate the old relationship from the one that you're currently developing as co-parents. Many tend to use "we have children" as a way to stay connected, which keeps them emotionally attached. There isn't a one way solution of communicating with your ex. I encourage you to be honest with yourself to know the season you're in to determine the proper way to deal with one another. You may not be in the best place to talk right now so the communication has to be at a minimum. Creating healthy boundaries will allow you both to make decisions that are in the best interest of the children.

Below are a few ways that you create healthy communication with the ex:

1. **Set limits on communication** – Keep the communication only about the kids. If you see that this isn't possible then text or use a co-parenting app to communicate such as Coparently, Our Family Wizard or Cozi. Email is also another way to keep a paper trail and keep it cordial.

2. **No "hanging out" or physical encounters** – This only creates confusion. It can give you hope that there's a chance for reconciliation when there really isn't. For the person who walked away, they

could be doing this due to guilt. This can also confuse your kids into thinking that eventually you all would be a family again when chances are that's not going to happen.

3. **Don't make the kids your messengers** -The kids need protection and sending messages through them only gets them involved in a way that's not their responsibility. If you can't talk, allow yourself to text, email or use the apps mentioned in #1.

4. **Your business is yours and his business is his** - What he's doing and who he's with really isn't a concern for you anymore. If you find that this is an issue where it's actually harming the kids and it's causing them to be emotionally unstable then bring these issues up to your ex or take further action (i.e. family attorney)

5. **Your "ex" is no longer your responsibility** – Therefore don't treat it as such. Sometimes we continue to treat our ex like a spouse. We lean on them too much for support or we allow them to lean on us too much. You don't want to "pretend" like you're something that you no longer are anymore. This could cause confusion and disappointment.

Ask yourself: Am I giving this person too much of myself still? Am I entertaining them a lot where it's keeping me from moving forward? Am I making myself available to this person as if I'm their wife when that is no longer my role with them? Will doing these things get me closer to my vision or pull me back from it?

Boundaries aren't always fun, but in order to divorce the story you must limit the communication. Limitations have a purpose and in this case, it's needed for you to deal with your emotions. These boundaries aren't to create strife or bitterness. They're in place to keep your foundation firm.

Why can't we be friends? Well no one said you couldn't. This isn't punishment for you or your ex, but being friends right now may not work. During this time focus on what's best for you, not him. This process is uncomfortable and also painful so to act like nothing has happened and just become friends right now may be unrealistic. In due time, you probably could have a very cordial friendship.

Thrive it out!

In your journal, answer the following question:

What boundaries will you set to communicate effectively with your ex?

Chapter 7

Divorce the Clutter

My mother is the kind of woman who loves to clean. I remember every Saturday morning we would get up and clean the house. My mom would get rid of things that she didn't need. According to her, everything has its place and she believed that if you no longer need it, what is the point in keeping it around? I inherited that same trait from my mom because I tend to declutter around twice a year. The goal is to always have less stuff and remove things I no longer need. I go through the kid's closets because they grow up so quickly and they have clothes and shoes that we can giveaway. I clean out my garage because, let's face it, the garage can be considered a storage area for many people and I just want to keep it to park the car. I go through the kitchen and the medicine cabinets, the pantry and even the storage bins. It's so simple to hold on to things that we no longer need, only to end up being tucked away and you find yourself saying, "I'll just deal with it later". We already know that later never really gets here. I'm not a fan of the labor of decluttering, but I am a fan of how I feel once it's done. I feel free, light, confident and accomplished. I feel like when I get rid of those old things, I can make room for things that are new.

There was a show that aired on television called Hoarders. The show was about people who lived their lives with so much clutter where it took over their personal lives. They were unable to detach themselves from even the smallest possessions. Their lives were packed and filled with things that they just could not let go of. I used to wonder, how someone could live like that? How can anyone live in so much clutter? Well, who am I to judge? It's hard to let go of things at some point and everybody and every situation is different. No one is the same and right now, during this season of your life, decluttering and getting rid of things can be extremely overwhelming for you. It could be that those things have a sentimental value. You might not even know where to begin. You could be fearful of letting things go or you possibly could be waiting for the right time. This book is about stretching you and making you uncomfortable. It is about doing things that you probably wouldn't have done if no one ever pushed you to. You may not "hoard" like the people who are on the show, but you could be hoarding things that can hold you back. Your house could be filled with memories of your marriage, memories of you and your ex-spouse, memories of you and your children with your ex as a family, the family traditions, and even some of the not so good times. You might be in a place where moving out is not something you can do financially or just prefer not to because you love your home. Decluttering is to make the space that we have comfortable and feel as much peace as possible. Your home is your sanctuary. It's your place of peace. What good is it to come home and not be peaceful? Your energy is extremely valuable and it comes from all sorts of things and that includes what's in your home. Remember you're building a new you and in order to bring anything better into your life, you must let go of those things that no longer fit. That includes physical belongings.

I recommend going through each room, cabinet, closets, the attic and even the garage. Tackling every room at one time may not be possible, but the most important room may be your bedroom. This could be the room that you spent the most time in with your former spouse. It could be filled with memories that could remind you of him that may put you in a mental and emotional space of hurt. Now it's time to make this "your' room. Decorate your room like you want it. Look at different colors that make you feel at peace again. Hang up pictures that are positive reminders of how beautiful and resilient you are. If you're having trouble with being creative, look online to find examples that can help you out such as Pinterest. Even if all you can do right now is get rid of old things, start there and progress into doing more. If you're having difficulty getting rid of something, ask yourself, "Is this useful for the next chapter of my life? What does this remind me of? Is it time to let go? How long has it been since I used this?"

What about your wedding mementos such as your gown, wedding album, wedding video, the ring or any keepsakes that reference your wedding day? That's a personal preference. No one can tell you to get rid of those mementos. They may still hold sentimental value to you. You may have children that would love to see their parents being together at that particular time in their lives. I would suggest not making those types of decisions based on current anger or even hurt because those feelings pass. You don't want to look back and say, "I hate that I did that."

These are a couple of things that you can do when it comes to your wedding mementos:

1. **For your gown** - You can save it. If you have a daughter, you can give it to her. Leave it up for her to decide. You could donate it to an organization or someone else who could use it that possibly cannot afford a dress.

2. **The wedding album and/or video** - You could keep the album for your children to see their parents in love during that season in their lives. However, if it causes you so much hurt, then you have to make the best decision on how you want to handle that. You can either keep it or get rid of it. There's no right or wrong way to handle this.

3. **The ring** - You could sell your ring, keep it for your child or you could just hold on to it until you decide on what you want to do.

Keep in mind that there are certain items that you probably will put a hold on at the moment. It's okay to do that. However, we want to start disposing of as many things that we can and start making room for the new life that we want to rebuild.

Operating with urgency avoids procrastination. Set a date to start and continue through other areas of the home, giving yourself a completion date for the project. Or, do one room at a time with a start and completion date. Get some storage bins and trash bags and see what can be donated or sold. Also, please inform your ex of the things he needs to get. If you feel overwhelmed, call up your friends to help.

Please note, if by any chance that you're in a legal process where it is undecided on who gets the home, please talk to your attorney about specific measures to take when it comes to your ex's personal belongings.

Get Your Finances in Order

When couples split, finances drop and it tends to hit women more than men. A woman's income drops about 41% and decluttering your home also means you need to extremely clear on your financial status. According to an article from Forbes Magazine titled *"6 Nasty Financial Surprises for Divorcing Women"* , one of those reasons is being unaware of marital debt such as the mortgage, loans, credit card debt, etc. Seven years ago I met a lady who was going through a divorce. Her finances were very tight from paying her car note, the mortgage, taking care of her kids and also putting food on the table. During this time she wasn't receiving any financial support for the kids from their father and the job that she had wasn't bringing in sufficient income. She mentioned that she received a letter in the mail about the property taxes on the home which stated that the taxes hadn't been paid in three years. This caused her to be blindsided by another bill. She mentioned that he took care of mostly everything so she wasn't quite clear on all the debt in the home which eventually became more than she could handle. She end up having to file for bankruptcy, foreclose on her home, and move back in with her parents.

Being unsure on where you are financially could make life after divorce more challenging than it has to be. During this time your emotions can be like a rollercoaster where it's causing you to not be conscious of your finances. You may find yourself avoiding your finances altogether because you're not ready to face reality, causing your bills to become overdue, which results in you being in more of a financial bind. You may be wondering, "How do I get started? I don't where to begin."or "This is all too much for me right now to handle." It may seem that way, but not doing anything isn't going to help either. We can learn anything in life. As a mom, I teach my children that if you don't know something then it's time to figure it out. The same goes for you. Don't use age or what has happened as your reason to not learn anything new. It's time to become a student and students learn. We often get discouraged when we're not clear on how to do something, but don't let that be your reason for not getting your finances in order.

Getting clear on where you are is what I call the "survival mode". This is the mode where you get all your paperwork and budgeting in order. This will give you clarity on where you are and also help you see what makes financial sense right now. Below are a list of steps to get started.

1. **Start Today** – No more waiting and believing that it can't be done. Many wait to start and when reality strikes, they get into a panic.

2. **Get Educated** – Remember, it's important to be a student now and getting educated will help educate you on money. There are plenty of free resources online such as podcasts, articles, YouTube, and even online courses. Also Google areas close to you that offer free tools and resources such as financial classes or programs for assistance where you can connect with a financial professional.

3. **Set a Budget** – Expenses change post-divorce and you don't want to spend more than you can afford. This will also allow you to be aware of where you are financially and if you need to scale back to pay off any debt, save and stay afloat.

4. **Update all Accounts** – Chances are you and your former spouse have things jointly from your bank accounts, credit cards, 401K, utilities, insurance

policies (health, life, homeowners, automobile) wills, trusts, property deeds, or other financial documents. Create a list and tackle them one by one.

5. **Credit Report** – You need to know what's on your credit to become aware of all of your debt. Get a free copy at https://www.annualcreditreport.com.

6. **Child Support/Alimony** – This tends to always be a sensitive topic however, kids aren't cheap and they have needs and it's important that those needs are met by the parents. You may be entitled to alimony. Make sure you see your family attorney for both.

Don't feel like this is impossible. You don't have to tackle everything today but you must start! If you need help, seek a divorce finance professional to help you get on track.

There's also a thriving mode that's not talked about enough because we're often led to believe that because you're no longer married and/or have become single parents that you have to struggle, that we will only live check to check, work two or three jobs for the rest of our lives to pay bills or limit ourselves on how much money we could make. If your vision statement doesn't include obtaining financial freedom, then you may want to revise it.

I know money doesn't make you happy, but let's just keep it real, it gives you options. It's a vehicle and it can do things that you couldn't do if you didn't have any. This can make a difference in how you and your kids live, the schools they attend, the things you can do and places you can go. It also can determine what you leave behind to your family. Let's face the reality, we all need money! The mindset you have around money matters. If you believe that you will only struggle then you will. Not because it's true but because that's your "believe" system. Earlier in the book I discussed the importance of having a believe system that will get you the results you want and having a poverty mindset will not create wealth for you.

When my ex-husband and I decided to separate, I lost my job two weeks later and eventually lost a total of five jobs in four years. This created a lot of financial stress for me, but it also developed a poverty mindset. I was so afraid of losing another job that I just settled for a job less than what I deserved. I remember when I went into that interview. I intentionally lowered my salary just so I could get hired because I was so afraid of not getting the job. I was so fearful that I could not pay the bills. My goal at that time was to get a job and keep a job. Not to mention, I believed that because I'm a single mother I was limited on how far I could go, even in the financial department of my life.

When it comes to thriving, it's about the long term and what you want to see happen. Divorcing your story is to understand that you do not have to struggle financially. Money is a resource and you need that to provide a means for you and your family. You don't have to live in poverty. You can live an abundant life. I want you to start thinking beyond where you are and ask yourself, "How can I thrive? How can I make more money? Can I get a better job? Do I need to go back to school and get that certification to get more money? Do I have a talent that I can open up and run as a business?" Many of us are sleeping on the gifts and talents that we have that could actually produce the income that we want.

Below is a list of things that you can start doing to help you go from a poverty mindset to a prosperous mindset.

1. **Set Better Financial Goals** – Where would you want to be in 5 or 10 years? Be specific with your numbers.

2. **Advance in your career** – You may be at a job that's not paying you want you're worth. It's time to start looking at where you are in your career and what it will take to advance to another level. Look at your job to see if there are any opportunities for advancement. Look for another job, or even take classes or courses that could make you more credible.

3. **What are you good at?** – Did you know you had a talent that you can offer as a service or product? Has anyone told you that you were great at something and you brushed it off? Chances are that could be your money maker. Making your own money is realistic and you're not exempt from it. You could do things like write an eBook or blog, create an online course, coach or train in a niche such as fitness or any field that fills a need. You can create shirts and sell them. The sky is limitless.

4. **Investing** – Look into Real Estate. There are plenty of women killing it! For example, Roberta Hoskie, a real estate guru who got pregnant at the age of 17 was living on welfare but she didn't let that stop her. At the age of 20 she bought a home through a first-time buyer program for $88,000 and within 5 years that same house was worth $300,000 and the rest was history. If she can do it then why can't you?

Financial Success Story

Valencia Morton who is now a money coach is known as "Millionairess Mama", shared her story with me on her financial journey to pay off her debt.

In 2015, when she and her husband decided that this was no longer going to work, she had 43K in student loans and credit card debt. She made a decision to move in with her mom to eliminate the overhead of maintaining a home on her own and created a budget to stay within her means as well as to scale back on any unnecessary expenses to pay off her debt.

She created eleven different ways to stream income from becoming a notary, selling items and even class action suits! In February 2018, she was able to pay off all her debt. Not only has she obtained financial freedom, she also created a business to help other mothers accomplish the same goal.

Will it be easy? No. Can it get done? Absolutely! There's nothing a woman cannot do when she has a plan!

Remember: The skies are limitless on how far you can go even financially.

Thrive it out!

What room will you start and when is the completion date? After that keep setting dates on the rooms you wish to tackle and the dates of completion.

What can you do to start getting your finances in order? (i.e. Budget, credit report, financial advisor, etc)

Chapter 8

Divorce the Ideal Story

"What happened?" is a question that many ask when you're going through a divorce. They want to know why it happened and what got you here. You could also be asking yourself the exact same question. Does the story you're telling matter? Absolutely! Especially the story you're constantly telling yourself. Are you telling the "ideal" story or are you telling the "real" story?

When I looked up the definition of the word ideal, it means "existing only in the imagination," meaning it's not real, it's what we imagined it to be. When I first told my story, I spoke from the ideal side of things. That was the story that made me stay a victim. This was the story of me "being the good girl who was done completely wrong" and him being "Mr. Bad Guy." This was the story that leaves out facts that could impact you. For a very long time, I loved that story because it made me look good and it made him look bad. However, the ideal story didn't get me anywhere because it allowed me to stay exactly where I was mentally and emotionally.

In order to divorce your story, you have to get clear on everything about it. Not only the part your former spouse played but the part you played as well. Only telling the story only from an ideal place is not a space that you can grow and learn from. This is the story that has the potential to keep you paralyzed therefore keeping you from seeing the relationship and its entirety. It's not the story where you get the chance to see where both people dropped the ball because as I tell people, just like it takes two individuals to make a relationship successful, it also takes two to make a relationship unsuccessful. I know sometimes that's a tough pill to swallow, but when you allow yourself to tell the truth, the whole truth and nothing but the truth, it will set you free.

The word "real" in the dictionary was described as true or actual. Telling the "real" story isn't always fun at all. This is the story that might sting a little bit, in fact, it might sting a lot. The real story leaves nothing on the table. This is the story that you may not want others to know because you may have some shame that goes with it such as something you've said, done, or overlooked. It could also have you saying "What was I thinking?" This might be the story that could have you in tears, but this is what you need. You need all the facts and evidence to make better decisions to heal properly and move forward.

I want you to think about going to court and taking an oath. When you take an oath in court, and if you weren't completely honest, chances are you could be charged with perjury. You can face legal consequences such as jail, probation, or even paying fines to the court. Even though you're not in a courtroom nor under oath, I want you to think long term about your future if you're not brutally honest about your story. Chances are you might end up in another relationship doing and going through the exact same things. You won't be able to get to the root of what you can repair to become a better version of yourself. You could find yourself playing the victim, becoming bitter, or holding a never ending grudge with your ex. Do you want to be that person?

This is how I stayed stuck in my story. There were just pieces of it that I didn't really want to discuss. I have to admit, I didn't really want to own the whole story and all the details of it. A lot of it had to do with guilt, pride, and feeling like a disappointment. Who wants to admit the part they played in something that didn't go right? There were things that I knew in the back of my mind, but I also knew that if I admitted it then that would mean it was true and I wanted to avoid that. I didn't want to feel wrong because I actually knew better, but I didn't do better. I didn't want to feel like, "How could I be so stupid?" Have you ever had a moment where you felt like, "What was I thinking? Why didn't I do this before?" That was me. Even though my ideal story was true to some level, it wasn't all the way true. I embellished on some things and it didn't allow me to thrive. In order for me to heal, I had to be able to face the truth of my relationship.

When I decided to own my truth by writing my story and leave nothing out, it made me see what I did wrong as well. Truth be told, I wanted to be the victim. I wanted to be the person who got saved because I was the good wife who cooked, cleaned, worked, paid bills, took care of the kids and the home. That part was accurate. However, there was another side of me that I didn't mention and that was the verbal disrespect that I used to give. It was the way I used to talk to him that was rude and out of order. My delivery was all wrong. I used to say things that I wouldn't want anybody to say to me. My vocabulary and my choice of words weren't really building him up. It was tearing him down. I used my mouth as weapon more than I did as a tool. It didn't have a filter and I didn't care at the time either. My defense on doing this was that he was constantly lying, staying out late, spending money recklessly all the time, not communicating, making decisions without me as well as other things. I felt that it justified my choice of words. My ideal way of thinking was that he deserved it! He should feel my hurt so that justifies what I do, right? No! Unfortunately it doesn't! My ideal story condoned my behavior which led me to believe that I had a valid reason for speaking the way I did. My real story could no longer excuse my behavior because that type of behavior doesn't just go away even if you're no longer with them. It carries over into other areas of your life and you'll always find yourself excusing a behavior that never worked.

My real story also allowed me to see signs before we got married that I chose to ignore. For example, my ex had a selfish streak in him and I noticed it to. It seemed like, if it wasn't beneficial to him, then it wasn't as important. The mutualism was off balance and I noticed it but I thought "Once we get married, it will change" or "Our love will fix this!" Why would I think that? Because I believed that I had enough power to fix and change him to be the man that I wanted him to be. When he wasn't living up to my expectations, it made me angry and frustrated. It caused me to lash out and say rude and disrespectful words. It also made me want to believe that he was doing me wrong when in reality, he never showed me this before we got married. I would say things like "He didn't appreciate me", "He didn't love me" or "How can he be so damn selfish?" but if none of that was shown before we got married then why believe it would be different? That was the part that killed me to admit but it needed to be done. When I decided to own that part as opposed to justifying it or operating from blame, I graduated from being a victim to a victor. This form of leveling up caused me to own my truth and the part that I played as well.

I often took pride in being the woman who did everything. From working, cooking, cleaning, taking care of the home, making sure all bills were paid on time, take care of the kids and helping him get his undergraduate's degree. You name it, I did it! Did he work? Yes, but the mutualism was off balance. This wasn't about both people doing the exact same amount, but this did reveal that the effort wasn't mutual. A huge part of me felt the need to overcompensate. There were a few reasons on why I did this.

1. I believed that the more I did, he would eventually return the favor.

2. I saw his mom do so much for him that it led me to believe that I needed to keep up and do the

same.

3. I thought he would love me if I did.

Seeing this made me understand that I was more of an enabler than a mate. Doing everything didn't make me a great spouse, it made me a frustrated, tired, and angry wife. I couldn't see this in my ideal story because it was being told from a place of receiving praise. This caused me to overlook the fact that I was making matters worse by believing that I was the victim because I did so much and there was a small level of reciprocity.

The "real" story isn't about justifying why you did what you did, neither is it about making excuses for anyone's behavior. The goal of telling the real story is to gain clarity on what really occurred, being vulnerable, developing transparency and gaining ownership. Earlier in the book I discussed ownership and how important it is to take responsibility and release the blame that you're placing on yourself and even your former spouse because this doesn't allow you to thrive. Accepting the story for what it is, is the only way you can move forward because you're operating from a place of truth.

Have you been telling the "ideal" story or the "real" story? Did you notice any red flags and decided to ignore them when they should've been addressed?

Did you see something that was there that you didn't want to allow yourself to face? Were you really "in love" or in love with the idea of it? Did you think if you spoke up about things that you didn't like, your ex would've left causing you to stay silent? Did your former spouse tell you what his needs were and you ignored them? Were you doing things or saying anything that may have come across very disrespectful during the course of your marriage?

Finding The Gaps

I had a client named Linda whose husband had an affair. One of the exercises we did was to write out the real story.

A few things came up. This wasn't his first affair. He cheated in a previous marriage, which she didn't know about. He addressed his needs to her, which she didn't pay attention to. She also avoided confrontation on issues that bothered her.

Did she deserve to be cheated on? Absolutely not! That's the part he has to take ownership of but there are some things Linda has to allow herself to see as well:

1. **She didn't do enough homework** - Infidelity is a big deal. Because this was done in a previous marriage, it's vital to know why this happened and what he did to see his wrong in order to take actionable steps to not do it again in another relationship. This goes to show that leaving a relationship and not doing the work that's required isn't the solution to everything.

2. **She ignored his needs** – Ignoring someone telling you their needs can be an indication for lack of respect. Men need respect and ignoring what he's telling you can make him feel disrespected.

3. **She never wanted to speak up** – Keeping the peace in the home doesn't mean to avoid what needs to be addressed. You can speak up on things that are an issue in a respectful way but ignoring the issue will become an even bigger one. Not addressing the needs of your spouse that can result in the relationship dying.

Linda is a nice and loving lady however, in order to prevent this situation from occurring in the future, she must acknowledge her own shortcomings in order to grow.

Thrive it out!

What are some things that happened that you're not allowing yourself to see? How was conflict typically resolved? What are some of the things that you just don't want to allow yourself to own because you may feel some shame, guilt or embarrassment?

Spend some time writing out your "real" story from the beginning. You may need to go as far back as when you all dated. This can be just between you and your journal. Fill up the pages if you have to but leave absolutely nothing on the table! There's no right or wrong. Own your truth!

As you grow and peel back layers, you will start seeing other things that you were unable to see before due to your emotional levels. You may not be able to see everything right now but as you grow and heal, you'll see more.

Chapter 9

Divorce Your View

When I was a teenager, my parents sent me to school to learn how to drive. Every time I would get in the car, my instructor always had me go through different things to make sure I had certain things in place before I started the car and pulled out of the driveway. I had to check my seatbelt to make sure it was fastened. I had to make sure my seat was adjusted to drive effectively. Most importantly, I had to check my rear view mirror and my side mirrors. He explained that the purpose of those mirrors were to mitigate any blind spots so that when I'm driving, I can prevent accidents from happening by being able to see what I probably couldn't see if I didn't have those mirrors. To sum it up, shifting those mirrors gave me a better view when driving. What if I never adjusted those mirrors? Chances are I wouldn't have been able to see the blind spots therefore becoming more at risk of getting in an accident despite my driving skills. I wasn't the only one on the road so it was important that I shifted my view to help me be a better driver. Shifting your view is a game changer, not just when driving, but also when allowing yourself to view your real story.

In the previous chapter you were told to write the real story. However, when you write the real story, you must also shift your view on it. Telling the real story can change your perspective such as how you see your former spouse, in order to gain a level of clarity that you didn't have before. When you write from an ideal place, you're not able to have this experience because you're only seeing it from one lens and viewing it from a victim's standpoint. Changing the lens and looking at it from the real story shapes you in becoming the victor. This lens will look at those "blind spots" that you couldn't see before. Before my real story was written, my lens were beliefs of:

"He didn't love me."

"He didn't care."

"He didn't think I was good enough."

"He's selfish."

"He's not doing his best."

You could be thinking the same way about your former spouse too right? I want you to develop a level of being open minded on why he could have been the way he was.

One of my initial blind spots was that our backgrounds were different. I was raised in a home where my parents have been married for almost 50 years and he was raised in a single parent home. I saw a model marriage my entire life. This isn't to say my parents were perfect either. For me, not making it work was never an option. My motto was, "Make it work no matter what and both people need to do all they can to make it work." That wasn't really his view on marriage. Divorce was always thrown in my face. I also didn't receive the support I needed from someone who was considered to be my husband. The leadership and the responsibility piece was extremely important to me. That standard I had of him as a husband was based on what I saw in my home growing up, even though that was never shown to me by him, neither was it a conversation we had. Allowing me to fully understand this and coming to the real story of the false expectation that I had of him was that he may have loved me, just not on a level that I needed. Maybe at that time that was all he could give. Did he really have an example of what leading a home looked like? I started to think, "Tonya, were you expecting him to be like your dad?" That hit me pretty hard, but to an extent I was because that's what I saw, that's what I knew and that's what I expected. This was a very important piece to understand because I don't want to repeat what I walked away from neither do I want to believe I can change someone. This isn't about the fact that he was in a single parent home and I wasn't. It was our views on marriage and relationships that was the issue. Can two people from two entirely different backgrounds work? Of course it can, but both must have a level of self-awareness in order to do what's required to make it successful.

After assessing how I used to speak to him, in my eyes that was my cry. It was my cry for love and attention. It was a call for my emotional needs that seemed to be ignored quite often. It was validation for my actions. My original philosophy was that "He did this so I'm going to do this!" I thought this would eventually make him hear me but it did the opposite. He just tuned me out. All that did was make me even angrier and more vocal! I didn't see it this way initially because the ideal story doesn't allow that. It wasn't until I told the real story that I could see this blind spot. I also mentioned earlier about how I saw signs and red flags. Instead of me saying "I was trying to make him better" to justify why he was doing me wrong or to make him seem like the bad person, my other lens was saying, "You knew this before it happened and even though you knew that he could do better and you know he had the ability to, that doesn't mean that he was going to. You took that risk on marrying him, knowing what he was giving you." Talk about a wakeup call! I had to give myself the same "tough love" that I give to others. The reality was that my ex was doing what I already knew he would do.

As a spouse, it's often told to take care of your mate. I'm on board for that but when there is no level of mutualism, a person can feel taken advantage of. For the longest time, that's how I felt. I even believed, that if I did more, he would see it and reciprocate, but it felt like the more I did, the less it mattered. When I examined this, I realized that I love to take care of the person I'm with but I also need that level of security in them as well. One of my blind spots in this was that I created a monster. I started enabling him too much where he didn't have a need to reciprocate because I never held him accountable to do so from the beginning. I thought that he would eventually just do it but it didn't happen that way. It would be great to think that many will just return the gesture but unfortunately, that's not always the case even when it's your spouse. I learned a few things from this:

1. Don't start anything that you don't want to finish.

2. Make your needs known even before you even get married. See how they respond to your needs. This doesn't indicate that a person can fulfill every single need, but you do want someone who's open to hearing you and making adjustments where they can.

Sometimes when we're telling our story, we will overlook blind spots. Those blind spots can symbolize perspective that will allow you to shift your initial view on the story. Originally, my story was very one dimensional that didn't do anything for me but stay in a vicious cycle of blame and anger. Changing my view changed my cycle to ownership and acceptance. Keep in mind that this isn't about justifying their behavior because sometimes we're hesitant on seeing things from a different lens because we believe that's excusing their behavior and we're letting them get away with it. It doesn't. The goal here is taking ownership and taking responsibility for what you've learned, gaining clarity on why they could be the way they are as well as why you were the way you were. Focusing on him and what he should've done is beyond your control. This is about controlling the only person you can and that's yourself. Remember: This is more about releasing the, "He owes me" mindset and welcoming the "I want to be free" mindset.

Thrive it out!

Have you allowed yourself to only look at it one way or are you allowing yourself to gain more understanding so you can get more perspective on the situation? What was your initial perspective? What is it about the story that will allow yourself to look at it from a different perspective? Then ask yourself, what other perspective can this become so that you can move forward and learn how to divorce your story.

Tonya Carter

Chapter 10

Divorce Unforgiveness

When I wrote my story, it was revealed to me that I had never really forgiven him. I used to say I did because I wanted to sound mature, but I knew deep down forgiveness has never been my strength. I always heard that you must forgive so you can move on, that it's for you and not the other person. That always went in one ear and out the other. I really wasn't trying to hear it. I used to think "How would forgiving them be good for me? They didn't deserve my forgiveness. If I forgave him, then he would think what he did was okay and I let him off the hook. How could I actually forgive and forget? I still have feelings on this, so how could I forgive?

One thing we all have in common is the ability to choose. We can either choose to do something or choose not to do something. Forgiveness was something that I never chose to do. It never was an option for me. I had already shut down the ability to not choose. What I realized was making the choice was the starting point. By making the choice, it allowed me to walk down the journey of learning how to forgive. Think of learning how to forgive like being a student. When you become a student, you take an interest in learning more about it. The more you learn about it, you become knowledgeable of it. Before you know it, you become a master of it because of the tools you've developed in this subject. Forgiveness was new to me and I needed to learn how to do it. For some people it is easy to come by, but for others it may not. I was one of those people. It just wasn't easy for me. I was a total grudge holder. However, because I made the choice to forgive, it opened up my mind, my heart and the possibility to learn how to do so. I wish I could say that once I made the choice, I forgave everything, but I honestly didn't. There were some things that I just needed to learn and understand to make this happen. Forgiveness is more than just a word. It's an action.

...BUT what if the "feeling" isn't right?

Have you ever said "I don't feel like doing this?" even though you know doing that one thing will make things better? That's how feelings work. Feelings are not always accurate. Let's face it, one day you might feel like doing something and then the next day you may not feel like doing anything. As I tell people, feelings and emotions are never to be overlooked, but it's important to never rely on feelings because chances are you won't make the best decisions for your life. This is about moving forward and thriving. It's about doing what you don't "feel" like doing but you know you need to do. It's about looking down at your vision statement and asking yourself:

"What would not forgiving do?"

"Will it change what has happened?"

"Will it help me moving forward?

Forgiveness is about being free. Many of us are emotionally imprisoned right now and we're held captive due to our current feelings. If you don't choose to release those feelings, your chances of being free are very slim. I know we're waiting on this feeling to be right to forgive. However, if that's what you're waiting on, then it's really unlikely to happen.

...*BUT they haven't apologized*

I know it might hurt that someone has mistreated you, verbally abused you, physically abused you, disrespected you, lied to you, cheated on you, stole from you and/or taken advantage of your love. I know some of us are really waiting on that apology because we feel like we deserve it. He owes us that. I felt the same way too because I thought that I needed him to see what he did in order for me to move forward. Do you know how much power that gives somebody over your life? Is that what you're doing right now? Are you waiting on that perfect apology? The words of, "I'm sorry for what I've done to you, will you forgive me?" in order for you to move on? Why are you waiting on someone else's action to determine your actions? Why would that be the determining factor on whether or not you should forgive?

When we're waiting on someone else to apologize, that's the control that we give them. That's what delays our healing process and stops us from moving on. Don't get me wrong, it's always great to receive an apology when it's genuine, but an apology only shows the other person's character and acknowledgement. It should never be the determining factor on whether you should move forward. Truth be told, some people would never see what they've done and even if they did, that doesn't mean an apology will be given. The harsh reality is they may never apologize. You might never receive the, "I'm sorry" that you believe you deserve and it's not really for you to understand why. The only why you need to understand is why it's important to forgive them even without getting the "I'm sorry" that you deserve. So instead of letting them decide on how you move forward, you decide how to move forward by realizing that healing is your responsibility and not theirs. Their apology should not be a requirement for you to move forward and it won't erase what has taken place.

Your health can't afford it....

According to Karen Schwartz, MD, Director of the Mood Disorders Adult Consultation Clinic at the John Hopkins Hospital, she mentioned in an article that forgiveness calms stress levels which leads to improved health. Schwartz also mentions that forgiveness isn't just about saying the words, it's an active process in which you make a conscious decision to let go of negative feelings whether the person deserves it or not. Holding on to anger can cause changes in your heart rate, blood pressure and immune response increasing the risk of depression, anxiety, heart disease, insomnia, as well as other conditions. When you release the anger, resentment and hostility, you begin to become calm and stress less, leading to improved health as well as feeling empathy, compassion and sometimes even affection for the person who wronged you.

Reading this article truly resonated with me because a lot of those health issues I started experiencing as well. Back in August of 2012 I experienced my first panic attack at my daughter's school. I never had one before and so I truly felt like I was about to die. I started getting really hot. My heart started pounding and I had the school call 911 because I didn't know what to do at that time with what I was experiencing. Needless to say, that wasn't the last one either. I used to wake up in the middle of the night and have them. I had them at work. I would walk away from my desk and go to the bathroom when I felt one coming. I started feeling anxiety and even depression. My body started feeling exhausted. It all just became too much. From losing five jobs in four years, finalizing the divorce, losing friendships, financial hardships, severe maintenance issues around the house, not having a reliable car, seeing my ex get remarried, being a single mother, owing the IRS, and losing my grandmother that year, it just seemed like it was a lot and being unforgiving did not help at all. It's funny because we really think that we can handle everything. We honestly believe our bodies are designed to take on all the problems and hold all the grudges. Carrying the weight on your shoulders is a lot more troublesome than letting it go. I started having chronic fatigue, migraines, joint pain, and even some immune issues. What's interesting is that before this all took place, I lost 80 pounds. I worked out and maintained a healthy diet believing that because I did so, my emotions would go away on its on and the anger I had would subside. There are benefits to working out but it wasn't the fix. You can never go wrong with working out and eating better, but your mind and body are connected and mine wasn't. Many say you are what you eat but our bodies also can become how we feel as well. I know we talk a lot about eating right and eating healthy, and you should, but what about the emotional and mental weight that some of us really don't talk about? We hold on to grudges believing that our bodies are unaware but your body feels everything, even the unforgiveness that you've been carrying around this whole time.

Initially, I wanted to believe that I forgave him. I used to say that to convince myself as well as others that I did but internally, I never did and I felt it too. That anger and resentment was still built up inside of me. I felt the rage and there's no amount of makeup, outfits, hairstyles, shopping, vacations or even another relationship that could take it away. I needed to release all negative feelings towards the situation because my health couldn't afford not to. Be careful when you say "people make you sick" because they physically can make you sick.

It's often easy to believe that it's a badge of honor to hold a grudge but in reality it's killing you more than it's helping you. 62% of Americans mentioned that they need more forgiveness in their lives. There are approximately 327.2 million people in America and 202,864,000 need more forgiveness in their lives. Are you apart of that 62%? If so, remember this: you're the one who's dying mentally, spiritually, emotionally and physically. In other words, in the end you're only hurting yourself, not them.

...BUT do we need to be friends?

If I forgive this person, does this mean we need to be friends? This isn't about being friends and restoring the relationship neither is it about being enemies. This is about your personal freedom and being free from anything that has hurt you that will stop you from moving forward. Truth be told, everyone doesn't need to be in your life. Some relationships are extremely toxic and need to be removed completely. Your real story and your healing over time can determine whether or not if you can communicate in the future, but in the meantime, it's okay to love people from a distance.

Communicating too much while healing can be confusing for you if not careful. It's important to have some level of boundaries during this time because you can find yourself prolonging your healing, still being physically involved, or hopeful of getting back together when that's not what he wants or that's not the best thing to do causing you more depression and hurt. If you have kids then of course you can't cut off all the communication, but don't believe because you have kids that you have to chat with them all the time as well. It's just important to know that you will always be in each other lives because you share the most beautiful joy that you all did create together and those are your kids. A new relationship has to be established. Depending on the season you're in, the communication may not always be the best. Chances are you both may be working on your healing and the conflict between one another can be on an all-time high. One parent may be cooperating, the other one may not. One might use the kids as a crutch, the other one may not which causes extreme conflict. Why does this seem to happen? Because the relationship you had as a couple is being spilled into the relationship as co-parents. However, forgiveness and healing will help this. Below are some tips to keep in mind while dealing with your ex and co-parenting during this time:

1. **Separate feelings** – As HARD as this could be, the relationship you once had as a couple should be separate from parenting. Treat this as a separate relationship.

2. **Keep the communication at a minimum** – Keep it short if you can't get along. Texting, email or using a co-parenting app can be used if best.

3. **Don't put your kids in the middle** – Don't make them responsible for passing on messages. This causes them confusion and the belief to have to choose.

4. **The kids' interest** – You may not be able to stand your ex right now but encourage your kids how important it is that they have a relationship with the other parent. Focus more on the kids and their needs than your own & allow your kids to determine the relationship they have with the other parent.

...BUT how can I forget?

I used to hear, "forgive and forget".... this was something that I had a difficult time digesting. How can you honestly forget what somebody has done to you? If someone verbally abused you, lied to you, physically hurt you, or cheated on you then how could you forget that? I don't think we can forget what somebody has done to us and completely erase it out of our minds as if it never happened. Sometimes I believe that's why many people don't forgive because they really don't think that they can forget and I agree, I don't think you can either. However, when I say don't forget, this isn't about putting your story on replay to remember & live in your hurt, it's about putting it on replay to move forward. Not forgetting can be a really powerful tool, it's all about how you use it.

1. It helps remind you to not go back to something that isn't good for you.

2. It teaches you what you don't want and what you do need.

3. It allows you to help others. Your testimony isn't just for you.

4. It makes you stronger. You develop a resilience within that you never would've obtained before. Strength is developed in struggles.

Forgiveness isn't about it never occurring in your life, it's about releasing the fact that you can't turn back the hands of time whether you choose to forgive or not. Ask yourself, " How can I make this pain work for my good?"

...BUT what about me?

There's a lot of discussion about forgiving other people as you should, but have you truly forgiven yourself? Have you let the things that has happened go? Forgiving myself was actually harder than forgiving other people. I was my own worst critic. I was harder on me than I was to others.

It was because I expected more from myself. There were times when I knew better, but didn't do better. There were times that I saw signs, but I chose to ignore them. I went away from my discernment and I knew that this was happening. I felt like I disappointed my kids, God and even myself. I'm that type of woman that felt like everything I touched needed to turn into gold. If it didn't turn out good then that meant I was no good. Due to my thought process, a lot of guilt, shame and failure traveled with me throughout my entire life. I had such a perfectionist mindset and I was much harder on myself than I was on other people. I believed that because it didn't work then that equated to me being a failure. I wasn't proud of everything I've done and I didn't think forgiving myself was something that I actually deserved.

Remaining a victim of believing that I couldn't be forgiven was tough. I treated my divorce like an everlasting punishment. Believing I was a failure in my marriage meant that I wasn't a good wife. I didn't do enough and I wasn't enough. I thought I was doing all I could do, but it still didn't work. Because my belief of marriage was so strong, being divorced felt like a death that I had committed. This type of thinking didn't set me free. This form of thinking kept me in a mental prison.

When you don't forgive yourself:

1. You keep reliving what you've done.

2. You don't make an attempt to make things better because you don't think you deserve better.

3. You struggle to forgive others.

4. You have difficulty trusting yourself.

The best thing you can do is to set yourself free. If a person you love such as your child, friend or family member came to you about something they were beating themselves up about, what would you say? Take your own advice for once. Stop placing yourself on a pedestal and give yourself that same level of grace and compassion that you would give to them. You're not perfect and you never will be. Take what has happened as a learning experience instead of a loss. After that, make the necessary adjustments to your life so you won't repeat what you don't want to experience again. Start shifting your focus on your vision and continue to take those necessary steps to get there. We often focus so much on regrets of the past that we don't preserve our energy for what we can change and that's the direction on where we're going. Your past has already been written and you can't undo what's been done. Your future still has pages to write but how you view yourself and forgive yourself will determine how those future pages will be written.

Forgiving others is wonderful, but when you open up your mind & heart to forgive yourself, it gives you the compassion to forgive other people because you realize that they are human just like you.

Thrive it out!

Ask yourself: Have I made the choice to forgive? Why is it so hard for me to do so? Do you I think that not forgiving them is helping me or hurting me? How?

Are you mentally imprisoned? Do you think you're not worthy of being forgiven? Are you holding a grudge against yourself because your marriage didn't work? Do you think that because the marriage didn't work, you failed as a person and you can't forgive yourself for it? What can you start doing to release yourself?

Chapter 11

Divorce Just Being a Teacher and Become a Student

Nothing made sense until I decided to become a student. Have you ever tried to tell someone something but they didn't want to listen? They didn't want to understand what you were trying to say? In the words of my mom, that would be considered a "hard headed" person. It takes a person who wants to learn in order to grow.

I remember back in school when we read books or were being told a story, one of the most important questions was "What was the moral of the story?" The moral of the story is a teaching or life lessons that is supposed to make you a better person. Based on the "real" relationship story that you've written, what did you learn? What was the moral of the story? Your story is your lesson and even though the marriage didn't work out the way you planned, you can always graduate when you've learned from the experience. There are always takeaways that you can utilize to thrive from this situation. If you go back and read your story, what did you honestly learn? Even if it's one thing, what is one principle that can be applied to help you thrive?

When I wrote my real story there were a few good things, but as I really examined it and I took my current emotions out of it, I realized that the marriage was based on what it could be and not for what it really was. One of my biggest takeaways has been that I can only change me. This might sound like common sense, but we all know that common sense isn't necessarily common practice. As much as I hate to admit it, I wanted to be an exception to the rule and I wasn't. Truth be told, I did see the best in him. I looked beyond what he was showing me to who I thought he could be. In the end, I realized that I was trying to change him into the person who I felt like he could be.

Initially, I didn't see this as a lesson learned because of the original mindset that I had. My thought process was "I just want to lift him up" and "I just wanted to encourage him." Some might ask, "Isn't that what couples do, make each other better?" Yes they should, but that has to be an invitation that must be accepted by both parties. I couldn't change him even if I felt like he wasn't living up to his best potential. Technically that was his job to want to and not mine to believe that I had the power to do so. In my eyes, I wanted to make him better, but in his eyes it seemed like I was nagging. The fact that we didn't look at this in the same manner, didn't turn out well in the relationship.

I really needed to get this! My mind was so fixed on "He didn't want to grow" which made the story not exactly true. Sometimes we feel that if someone doesn't do what we think they should do, it makes them not appreciate us. Now that could be true, but not entirely. That's basically saying, you only appreciate me if you do what I want you to do. That's a very false expectation of anyone and it could prevent you from learning the lesson, therefore, believing the ideal story as opposed to the real story. Get deep on this and not just give a surface level response. Don't say things such as "I've learned to not love or trust again or to never marry someone like this again." Get very clear and specific on the lessons and the experiences because this is what will give you clarity on your relationship. To divorce your story is to understand the lessons, because if not you'll take this as a loss.

Thrive it out!

Ask yourself: Based on the real story, what were the facts? What were the lessons that I can take from the story? As you continue to heal, you may learn more.

Helpful Tip Go back and reread your story, multiples times if needed. If you left something out...write it out.

Chapter 12

Divorce Unloving Yourself

Have you ever heard the saying: "You have to love yourself more" or "You can't love another person until you love yourself first?" I heard that quite a bit, whether it was on social media, in an article or a book I've read. It's actually something that I've told other people before too. As I thought about it, I really didn't love myself like I thought I did. I would say it, quote it, and even tell other people to do it but I didn't. From the outside my life looked like I loved myself. You saw pictures on social media, supposedly living my best life, spending time with my children. I worked hard, I did all those things but deep down I just wasn't feeling myself. From the insecurities, the belief of not feeling like I was enough, feeling like I was a failure, the past experiences, the things I settled for and even relationships that

I entertained, I didn't resemble a woman who loved herself.

When I looked up the definition of the word self-love, it meant an appreciation of one's own worth or virtue that grows from actions. It begins when we observe our actions and words with compassion as if we were our own best friend. When you develop self-love, you're able to accept your strengths and your imperfections. When you ask a person, do they love themselves, the politically correct answer would be yes. However, based on the definition, is it safe to say that you have been your own best friend? Do you have an appreciation of your own worth? Have you embraced your strengths as well as accepted your flaws? Do you praise or punish yourself? Only you know that answer. Only you know deep inside how you feel about yourself and the best way to really answer that is to examine the relationship you've established within.

If loving yourself is something we should do, then why does it seem like it's so hard to do? For many, it's because of how we perceive self-love to be. Self-love is actually a lifestyle. It's the way you live and I'm not talking about in a monetary way. I'm talking about in a day to day way. We often confuse loving ourselves with consumerism. As for me, I didn't love myself like I thought I did because I acted on my feelings rather than my state of being. Earlier I mentioned the things I did that looked like I loved myself but those were just moments that led me to believe for a while that I did. During those times of going out and treating myself, it felt good, but afterwards I wasn't feeling my best. I was using consumer self-care as a way of me loving myself when that's not a true indication of self-love. This wasn't about not hanging out with my friends or never having fun, it's more about not using this as a cover-up for how you really feel.

Many of us have been programmed to believe that loving yourself is selfish. You're taught that your needs don't matter and that you should make everybody else the priority while you're left being the option. In many families, a woman's experience is that everybody's needs and wants comes before her own, and doing anything else outside of that is very abnormal. I came to the conclusion that doing this made me angry because I was looking for other people to fill my cup because I was pouring out to everybody else. I thought this would make others considerate of me and my needs and they would reciprocate by giving me what I was giving to them but that wasn't the outcome. No one else was responsible for filling my cup but myself and because my cup was empty, I knew this was going to take work and most importantly a new way of believing that this wasn't a selfish act. In the beginning it felt weird doing this because this wasn't my norm, but like they say when you're on an airplane before takeoff, you have to put the oxygen mask on you first then you're able to take care of everyone else.

I also thought that in order for me to love myself, certain things needed to be in place in order for me to embrace self-love. I operated out of the mindset that something had to take place in order for me to me happy. Have you ever said things like: "Once I get this, I'll be happy?" or "Once this happens, I'll be happy." Some of us are waiting for that relationship to make us feel worthy of love or maybe waiting on that job to acknowledge what we do or even keeping people around at the expense of who we are because we often allow how others think and feel about us to determine our value. In other words, until we get the validation we need from others, we will continuously minimize who we are and how we feel about ourselves. Always know, your first validation shouldn't come from others, it should come from you. When you operate from a place of self-love, the need for others approval diminishes.

Many of us also experience difficulty loving ourselves because we focus too much on past situations. I initially allowed my divorce to shape how I felt about myself. Thoughts of failure and not feeling good enough allowed me to operate from a negative place of not embracing self-love. Right now you're going through a divorce or you may be divorced, and you could be looking at yourself as a failure, a person who's incapable of keeping a marriage together, or a person who feels like they're worthless because they're no longer attached to someone. You also may have experienced other situations from your upbringing that have made a huge impact on how you believe and think about yourself. It's often said "Leave things in the past" but they're often brought into the present which travel with you into the future.

I want you to say this out loud "I am the most important individual in my life." It might sound a little awkward saying this, because chances are you've never seen yourself to be the most important person in your life. Everything in life does start with the relationship that you've established within yourself. Divorcing your story involves you developing a deep love and appreciation for who you are. Its understanding that loving yourself is unconditional and not on conditions. It's appreciating who you are at this present moment while continuously working on becoming the best version of you. It's realizing that it's not selfish to make you a priority. It's recognizing that who you are is enough and you don't need validation from others to feel validated. It's understanding that this experience doesn't disqualify you as a person who can't love themselves. It's not an appointment on your calendar. It's a daily 24/7 appreciation that you have for yourself no matter if you're out or at home. Always know, you are loved.

Thrive it out!

What do you believe about yourself? What do you say about yourself? Are the things you're doing an example of you loving yourself? Will these thoughts and actions get you to your vision?

Chapter 13

Divorce Being Inauthentic

If you were to be asked, who are you, what would your response be? One of my biggest struggles was not really knowing who I was outside of being a mom, someone's wife, daughter, cousin, friend, niece, aunt, even a college graduate. I was still unsure. When we're asked who we are, we start going into what we do. In order to define our identity, we say things like:

"I'm a docter."

"I'm a lawyer."

"I'm an accountant"

"I'm a mom."

"I' have a Master's degree."

"I'm an entrepreneur."

"I'm a wife."

However, the question is: "Who are you at your core?" Who are you without the labels? Would you still feel like you're relevant if you didn't have those labels or do you only feel significant when you attach yourself to something or someone? My labels were what I used to define who I was.

In the midst of all those labels were coverings of who I was at my core. A lot of those labels that I was attached to allowed me to conform to be somebody I never was from the beginning. I never used the voice that I had inside of me to my fullest advantage. My voice was gone. That voice of being my authentic self. The voice of being who I was unapologetically. When I was a wife, I conformed and tolerated things that I said I would never tolerate under any circumstances. But to keep the title of being a wife, I intentionally minimized my voice. There was a part of me that wanted my parents blessing more than I wanted my own so I went to school for something I never truly wanted to do which caused me to minimize my voice. I was often asked by many, "Why do you act like that?", "Why do you always have an opinion?" or I was told, "A woman shouldn't always voice her opinion, that's not what a lady does." This made me believe that I needed to conform to make others comfortable. I had to be a certain person to the world in order to be accepted, which caused me to lose my voice. When my divorce happened, it made me angry because as I looked at my life, a lot of things didn't turn out as planned because they weren't my plans to begin with. They were everyone else's plans that I allowed myself to adapt to, causing me to lose my voice. There I was being someone I never wanted to be, believing that if I did what others wanted of me, my life would turn out fine. How was that ever going to happen if I wasn't being my authentic self to begin with? It was time that I stopped being what everyone else wanted of me and be who I was created to be.

Loving yourself requires you to be who you are, authentically. You have to know who you are from the inside and you also have to love yourself from the outside. I love Maya Angelou's poem, *"Phenomenal Woman."* That was a poem that she wrote to herself and for other women to embrace who they are, as they are. Maya Angelou experienced hardships as a child. Her parents divorced and she was also raped at the age of eight by her mother's boyfriend. When her uncles found out, they beat him to death causing Maya to silence her voice for years because she believed her voice got him killed. As Maya started to regain her voice with the help of a teacher, she studied authors such as Charles Dickens, William Shakespeare, Douglas Johnson and James Weldon Johnson. From these experiences emerged a woman who won a scholarship to dance and act as well as record poetry. She became pregnant at the age of 16 which caused her to put her plans on hold for a while but was discovered by a theater group from a job she had at the nightclub. Maya went on to travel the world writing and acting in plays, writing poetry, articles, screenplays and producing as well as so many other things. I truly believe that she wouldn't have been one of the most influential women of all time had she not allowed her light to shine. It was through these adversities that she found her authentic self. Maya's voice was through her words and her writings. She realized that who she was is enough, and she used what she had to allow herself to show up to the world.

She said in her poem:

Pretty women wonder where my secret lies.
I'm not cute or built to suit a fashion model's size
But when I start to tell them,
They think I'm telling lies.
I say,
It's in the reach of my arms,
The span of my hips,
The stride of my step,

The curl of my lips.
I'm a woman
Phenomenally.
Phenomenal woman,
That's me.

I walk into a room
Just as cool as you please,
And to a man,
The fellows stand or
Fall down on their knees.
Then they swarm around me,
A hive of honey bees.
I say,
It's the fire in my eyes,
And the flash of my teeth,
The swing in my waist,
And the joy in my feet.
I'm a woman
Phenomenally.

This poem is a reflection of a confident woman who embraces what she has as opposed to being concerned about what she doesn't have. Her uniqueness was her inner confidence that showed up externally to the world. She embraced her hips, her presence when walked into a room, and the inner mystery that many wouldn't understand. She embraced that her words can impact and influence others and change lives. It's only when you can fully appreciate who you are and how you are to live that you can be your authentic self. Do you feel like you're enough? Have you minimized who you are to belong? Do you feel like how you look isn't enough for people to accept? Do you believe that if you showed up to be who you are, that people will accept you?

From the beginning, I was a fiery little girl. I always had an opinion. I always had something to say. I didn't like doing what everyone else was doing. I liked walking to the beat of my own drum. I always had a different mindset than many people and because others may not understand how you think and how you operate, you feel like who you are isn't who you're supposed to be and because of that, I had trouble understanding that I was enough. When others question why you are the way you are and why you shouldn't be like that, if you haven't developed a self-love for yourself, it leaves you to question the same thing.

I didn't want to be an outcast so I minimized my voice. That fire that was once lit had started to dim. I thought being bold and being honest was an issue because we live in a world where many people aren't that bold. They'll rather be liked by others where it compromises them loving themselves. We live in a world where people aren't that honest because living in your truth almost seems wrong. Everyone has a voice. Our voices might be different, but that's what makes our voices unique and that's what makes them matter. I have a place in this world, and you have a place in this world too. What makes me unique is appreciating that my boldness and my honesty is just a part of who I am. I recognized that being anything outside of that was causing me to operate from a place of inauthenticity therefore leaving me unfulfilled and with no voice.

Have you lost your voice? Have you been authentic to who you are or authentic to others to make them feel comfortable at your expense? Do you believe that who you are wouldn't be acceptable for the people who you want to be in your life? Being your authentic self comes with a price that many don't want to pay. It comes with being able to handle the fact that everyone (even the ones who are close to you) may have an issue accepting the unique version of you. They may not understand but it's important to know it's not for everyone to understand. This is YOUR life and it's essential to know that this is the only life you have so why not be who you're supposed to be? Why not let your own light shine? Even though everyone might not get it, the reward will be high! You start showing up more bold and courageous. You won't compromise who you are to make others comfortable, you realize that you're important no matter what label you have or don't have attached to you. Everybody's not going to be able to accept or appreciate the unique you but how do *you* feel about you? Are you willing to keep giving yourself up for the sake of others? Are you willing to be inauthentic to be accepted? Or are you willing to be bold and shine? Divorcing your story is to understand that who you are is enough for you to get where you need to go.

Thrive it out!

I want you to look at your vision statement that you wrote in the very beginning and ask yourself: Have I been shrinking myself at the expense of others? In what areas have you been downplaying who I am? How can I get there if I'm not being who I am? How can I get there if I keep my voice on mute? How can I get there if I don't embrace my uniqueness? Outside of my birth name and labels, am I aware of who I am?

Chapter 14

Divorce Negotiating

One of my favorite companies is Discount Tire. I consider it to be the "Chick-Fil-A" of tires. I don't go anywhere else to get my tires or have them rotated and balanced. The reason is because I love the service. It doesn't matter which location I go to, I get the same level of great customer service. I often wondered, why certain companies have this standard while many don't. What's the secret? One thing's for sure is that they live within their core values. I spoke with a manager at one of the locations and he shared that the owner who just recently passed away really had a deep care for his people and his work. He also had certain standards that were required for all employees. In order to be a store manager it was mandatory for them to read his book to get an understanding on how the company was built. The owner had values that were established within himself that crossed over into his business. His connections to the community and building healthy relationships mattered. He believed in respect and fairness and the willingness to pay it forward. These values resulted in 975+ locations in 34 states. They are also known to be the nation's most trusted tire and wheel retailer.

I want you to think about your core values like a business. Business core values should guide all your company decisions. It helps to decide on hiring a candidate that cannot only successfully do the work, but also fits within the core values of the organization. It also helps businesses make decisions that will help the company grow but not in a way that takes away from their beliefs. It also keeps companies in business a lot longer due to the foundation that was set which was based on their values versus other companies that frequently compromise their morals for the sake of money. Earlier in the book I mentioned that you are a personal brand. You are the CEO of you. In order to be that personal brand that thrives in life, you have to establish core values for yourself. Your values are standards that you live by that will help you navigate through life in a way that will set you up for success professionally and personally. Your values will help you choose better relationships, help you not to settle and most importantly determine how you should treat and value yourself. These are principles that come before anything else, no matter how good something or someone appears to be, in other words, your values are necessary for an intentional and fulfilling life.

For core values to be meaningful, you must live in them as well. For instance, if loyalty is a core value, then not only should you look for that in others but you should also be living in a way that exemplifies what being loyal looks like. When you don't live by your core values, you'll find yourself living on other people's terms to settling for something that you know is beneath you. This could cause bitterness, anger, and even sometimes resentment. If you do this long enough, it will make your life seem meaningless and unfulfilling.

Why does living in your core values matter? Because they are your driving forces that direct you to live an intentional life. You'll make decisions off your core values rather than what appears to look good. You also realize what's important and what isn't. When you have certain core values, everything doesn't matter and you start making what's important the priority. It allows you to show up daily in a way that matches your belief system and it also allows you to be aware of making adjustments within yourself in order to stay within your core standards. You develop your own happiness as opposed to relying on other people to make you happy. You start building confidence because you're striving to live to be your authentic self. You set better goals because they're in alignment with who you are. You start regaining your power because you're developing a culture of choosing you as opposed to waiting on yourself to be chosen by others. Your core values are your commandments that define who you are and what matters to you as a person.

I didn't live by my core values all the time and it caused me to make worse decisions. I made bad choices with men. I made financial decisions that weren't so good. I settled for everything from corporate jobs that I never wanted just to get a paycheck to even doing certain things that I knew wouldn't make me a better person. I lived by my values sometimes or I revised them to fit something or someone, which in the end left me upset and hurt. It created a deeper depression for me and caused me to be extremely disappointed. I wasn't disappointed in other people. I was disappointed with myself because I knew I was going against what I knew I should have never done. Your core values are not a contract, they're a covenant. When I was married, I was willing to make a covenant to someone else, but I needed to make a covenant with myself first. My covenant was never to be compromised or even negotiated because one core value compromised is one core value too many.

To divorce your story is to understand that your core values are not something that you just say, but something you do by living by them and walking away and turning down anything that will go against what you believe in, no matter how challenging it is to do so.

Thrive it out!

Take some time to reflect on your values. What are they and keep them simple. What value(s) have you compromised that have left you disappointed? What has compromising your values done to you emotionally, physically, financially and/or spiritually? Can your vision come into fruition when you don't live in them?

Tonya Carter

Chapter 15

Divorce the "Fixed" Mindset

I'm the proud mother of a 16 year old son and an 12 year old daughter. There have been several times that when they get challenged to do something that pushes them beyond where they are. They tend to freeze up, believing that they can't do it or they don't have the ability to learn it. As a parent, my job is to encourage them as well as teach them that you can really do whatever you set your mind out to do. Those are great positive words but without action the words are not as meaningful. That same level of encouragement that I have pushed continue to in my children, is something I needed to do for myself as well.

Carol Dweck is known for her research in motivation, personality and development. She mentions in her book *"Mindset: The New Psychology of Success"* that there are two types of mindsets. A person either has a "fixed" mindset or a "growth" mindset. A fixed mindset is an established mind. It's a mindset that believes you can't go any further than where you are. It's a static mind that believes how you think is how you think and you can't think of anything else besides what you're currently thinking. A person with this kind of mindset avoids anything that challenges them. They don't give themselves time to learn and understand so they give up easily. They don't believe that effort will take them further. They don't like any feedback that will help them because they view it as critical and they believe other people's success minimizes theirs. This kind of mindset causes a person to plateau and not reach their fullest potential.

The growth mindset is where a better mindset can be developed. A person takes on challenges and embraces them. They view obstacles as opportunities. Instead of being scared of the unknown they're willing to take the road less traveled. They take criticism as a way of positive feedback to learn and they view others success as an inspiration to keep going. The great thing about this mindset is that it's not "either you have it or you don't," you can always choose to create a mindset of growth.

I juggled between both mindsets but I often fell under having a "fixed" mindset. I realized that I limited myself a lot on how far I could climb because of what I experienced. I placed a lot of limits on myself because I believed that what I had, what I've experienced, how I felt about myself, and what I knew was limited. I was so busy proving my philosophy on life to be right that it left me being fixed to believe that this is what I had to work with. I didn't like getting feedback from others because I believed that it minimized my intelligence. The love that I established within myself was an indication of my success in life both personally and professionally. When I experienced losing five jobs in four years and becoming a single mother of two, I purposely settled for a salary less than my worth just to "secure" a job. My motto was "Girl, you gotta do what you gotta do!" That's true but not to the extent of believing you have to settle. I remember sitting in an interview and downplaying my salary. I wanted a job so bad even at the expense of compromising my worth in the marketplace. The belief of failure from divorce and my own inner self worth created a fixed mindset that I couldn't have the relationship that I desired, causing me to deal with a "situationship." I not only compromise my values but held the belief system that this was all I could get.

Developing a growth mindset has been rewarding. It has definitely had its challenges but I had to tell myself the same thing I tell my kids: "You can do whatever you set your mind to." It was important that I become my own cheerleader and give myself that same level of encouragement that I give to others. Developing this mindset took work from reading books, connecting and building relationships with people who had a growth mindset, being honest with myself and pushing through from what I used to consider a "fixed" belief.

Oftentimes, we see people at a certain level in life and we feel like they're lucky. No one is lucky and no one is free from problems. Everybody goes through some level of adversity in their lives, but what makes people different from others is the fact that they didn't allow their mindset to be fixed. In other words, they didn't let what happened to them be their indication on how far they could climb. They didn't place limits. They didn't say, "Because I've been through this experience I can't achieve what I wanted in life." Instead they said, "Because of this experience, this is going to push me to get those things that I want out of life."

To love who you are at your highest, it will involve establishing a growth mindset. Growth says, "I have the ability to learn more than what I know." It says, "Even though this happened to me, this isn't the final chapter of my life, it's just a chapter in the book of my life." There are plenty of women that are doing it for themselves.

They are choosing to thrive after a relationship doesn't work out. As long as you place limits on how far you can travel because of what you've experienced, you won't allow yourself to move forward. If you let what somebody else has done to you be a positive driving force, then you develop the growth mindset to thrive.

Thrive it out!

What mindset do you operate in the most? What areas in your life do you categorize being "fixed?" What "fixed" beliefs must be changed to a growth belief to get to your vision?

Tonya Carter

Chapter 16

Divorce Your "Singleness" View

We're often led to believe that being single is a disease that nobody wants to catch. We feel less than because we're not tied to a relationship. We believe that if we're in a relationship that we've made it to some level of worthiness as if we weren't worthy when single. When you're single, you get questions or statements like "Where your man at?" or "Something must be wrong with you because you're single." This can cause you to believe that you're only relevant if you're in a relationship. This kind of mindset can lead you down a path of destruction, causing you to choose a mate out of desperation rather than inspiration. I'm not here to tell you to not desire a relationship, but it's important to know that a huge part of having a successful relationship with someone is to first develop a successful and healthy relationship with yourself.

A few years ago, I remember having lunch with a friend of mine. He mentioned that since his divorce, he realized that he never "decluttered" his life. He went on to say that since his divorce he's always been in a relationship playing "husband" to a girlfriend and never took the time to embrace his singleness. In my mind, I was like "Wow!" He's a successful guy, has written books and traveled the world however he still doesn't feel like he's whole. This goes to show that you shouldn't attach the level of your wholeness to what you do.

We're not really taught a lot about being successful at being single. We're not trained to embrace who we are as an individual and learn to be whole before we're in a relationship. 42% of first time marriages end in divorce. 60% of second marriages end in divorce and 73% of third marriages end in divorce. When you look at these stats, you would think that if you get married a second or even a third time, the numbers will decrease however, the numbers seem to go up the more times you get married. I don't know all the answers as to why this happens, but one thing I do know is that many people do not discover who they are before they allow themselves to be attached to someone. There's a book titled, *"Single, Married, Separated & Life after Divorce"* by Dr. Myles Monroe. He mentions in his book, "People do not have a singleness problem. They have an entirely different problem and that's called being single."

This book goes more in detail about being single and how we have defined it all wrong. When you look up the definition of the word single, its synonyms are "individual, separate, distinct, unique and whole." As Dr. Myles Monroe states in the book "Will there ever be a time, and has there ever been a time, when you cease to be "separate, unique and whole?" Think about this: who would want to be a half person? Who would want to stop being their unique and whole self? Being single has been described as this "awful" relationship status when it shouldn't define who you are based on who you're with. For many generations and from family, friends, social media, relationship experts and even the church, being single just hasn't been something that was taught to be embraced. It's as if being single is some form of humiliation causing one to feel hurt, unworthy, and even rejected.

Dr. Monroe also asks "Does getting married do away with this definition of being single?" "When you marry, do you stop being a single individual who is unique and whole?" Well you shouldn't. Being in a relationship shouldn't require you to give up your wholeness, neither should it cause you to wrap your entire identity into who you're with. What I often hear from many women who suffer from a divorce is, "I lost myself and I don't know who I am." or "Who am I without them?" These thoughts tend to occur when you haven't found yourself prior to the relationship. It could also be because you've never given yourself permission to be that person that's already inside of you.

A lot of the anger I felt from my divorce came from me not being who I wanted to be. I thought I needed to be this certain kind of wife to make my relationship work. even at the expense of me going against and compromising on things I never wanted to agree upon. From the beginning, I always felt like there was more I needed to accomplish in life but all of that had to be put on hold because I was now a wife and a mother. Doing this caused me so much irritation because not only did the relationship not turn out as planned, I also felt like I gave up so much of myself that I never wanted to, causing me to have some level of resentment towards my former spouse. I know it sounds noble and commendable to give up so much of yourself for the relationship but does that really work? Does that make the relationship successful? Does it make both people satisfied or is it a one-sided satisfaction?

I didn't know who I was before I was a wife. I thought I knew who I was because of what I had. Yes I had graduated from college, had a job, took care of the home and family but I was still a "half" person. I was unsure of my values and my inner worth because of what I tolerated, compromised and placed on hold. Knowing who you are should be a prerequisite before you get involved with anyone. When you find who you are, you're not willing to lose that person. You're not willing to go against your values. You also know that who you're with doesn't define who you are and it's not their job to bring you a level of happiness that you haven't acquired within. On my healing journey, I decided to go on this discovery of finding her and studying me. I had to ask questions such as: What did I give up that I knew would take away from who I am? What did I compromise on that took away from my values that's needed to be a successful and whole individual? What did I always want to do but never allowed myself to take action on because I was a wife and a mother? Was I ever a successful single? Did I ever have a level of self-love before I was married or was I looking for my marriage to give me that?

I came to the conclusion that I never had the opportunity to embrace my singleness. Because I got married so young and started a family, there wasn't a moment in my adulthood that I took the time to really get to know me. Not only did this cause me to not discover my own voice, I didn't know who I was to my core. I didn't have a self-love within so I was seeking that in other places. Truth be told, there was a level of inner happiness that I hadn't obtained yet. If I wasn't authentic and joyful as a single person then why expect authentic relationships? Finding who you are and walking that journey takes courage. You're unraveling who you thought you were supposed to be to who you were created to be. You're facing those "ugly" truths about yourself that you never wanted to confront such as your insecurities that could be holding you back. You come to a place of acceptance that you weren't a successful single before you got married. You realize that you haven't been living up to your fullest potential because you placed everything on hold for everyone. You understand that no one is responsible to make you happy, a person should only be an addition to the happiness that you've developed within. Your view on being single has to change. You recognized that single doesn't mean "half" neither does it mean you're less than. You're no longer looking for someone to complete you. You know that this is a time for self-discovery and knowing and loving the most important individual in the world and that is yourself. Does this mean you need to be perfect? No, but it does mean that you need to be as whole as you possibly can because when you've worked on yourself, you will not lose her for anything or anyone again. Divorcing your story is understanding that being single is deeper than just a relationship status, it's a time of self-discovery, establishing trust within and enjoying life in your individual wholeness.

Are you ready to date?

One of the biggest myths of getting over a relationship is to get in another one. During this time, you could be extremely vulnerable and you might not be aware of it. When your emotions are high, your vision isn't as clear which could cause you to not have as much clarity as you believe you do. Even if walking away was the right thing for you to do, this doesn't dismiss the fact that it did have an impact on you. I thought because our divorce was mutual that I wasn't hurt, but I wasn't fully honest with myself either. I was hurt because I hated that the relationship got to this point. I was damaged by the things that occurred in our marriage. I was still emotionally broken. When I went out and started dating, I realized that I didn't allow myself to heal and that put me in a position to not truly understand the dating game and the playbook. This isn't about playing games, but it is about understanding the game of dating.

Unfortunately, everyone isn't who they claim to be and because of the lack of knowledge I had and the lack of healing on my part, it caused me to develop a situationship. For those who are unclear on what a situationship is, it's a relationship with no title but more than friends. I met a guy that I really did like, at least I thought I did at the time because he looked and appeared to be somewhat different than what I was used to. He definitely made me laugh, we could talk for hours, and he was physically attractive. It was never a dull moment when we were around one another. It seemed like we had so much in common. It felt to be a connection between us at that time but that wasn't enough to sustain something serious. During this time he wasn't really serious about me. I was just a person of convenience. I was the person that he liked to talk to, but only on his time. When I would bring up issues that I had when it came to us, there was never a level of compromise. He made promises that he didn't always keep which was a concern for me but I found myself overlooking it. I allowed the "decent" things he had in him to overshadow what mattered long term. He was the kind of individual that as long as it worked for him, it didn't matter who it impacted. He had some good traits, but our values were so different that in reality, this wasn't going to turn into anything more than what it was. Foolish of me to think it was ever going to be. I was very naive during this time, because I hadn't been in this dating game and I wasn't aware that this is what some people were doing. In my eyes, this was going to be more, in his eyes, it was nothing more than what it was.

He decided to stop dealing with me and I was very hurt. During this time, my divorce was final and I had lost my third job. Talk about feeling like a loser. All this did was put me in a deeper state of depression because I felt like I was losing. Here I am with a marriage that didn't work, a third job loss, and this guy who I thought would be with me...failed. As I look back and reflect, I didn't know where I was with my emotions because during that time, I realized that no one ever really taught me to deal with my emotions. They were all screwed up. I thought by being so strong, my emotions would just go away on their own, or that I could repress them and it wouldn't impact me, but they did. I was covering up my hurt by attempting to be with someone. Not only did this allow me to choose out of hurt and desperation, it also left me feeling rejected and depressed.

Take inventory on where you are with your healing and understand that everyone isn't going to be compassionate towards what you're going through right now. You may think you're ready to date but when you go out there and meet someone and tell your story be cautious because unfortunately people can use that against you. They see that you could be vulnerable. They notice that your emotions are raw and they can also tell if you might be in a position of desperation for love. If you know internally that your emotions are raw, you are extremely vulnerable and you could possibly do something that will not only cause a delay in your healing, but potentially involve yourself with someone who isn't suitable for you. My advice for you in this season is to not date right now.

When I date someone, I want to get to know them. I like to understand them and see life in their lens, but oftentimes we don't know ourselves on this same level. This may sound unconventional but I recommend that you date yourself. Get to know and spend some time with yourself. Know your likes and your dislikes. Enjoy your alone time. If you're unable to do that, you haven't elevated to embracing your singleness. You'll be surprised at how many people are codependent. When you get to a place of enjoying your alone time, you're not so concerned about having to be in a relationship so desperately where you feel forced to choose anybody. Get clear on what your values are and most importantly walk and live in them. Don't say what you want out of somebody that you're not doing with yourself every single day. This is how you find yourself back into another relationship that doesn't compliment you. We tend to believe that the romantic relationship we're in determines our worth but I beg to differ. It's the relationship that we've developed with ourselves first that does.

Look inward and ask, "Am I in a good emotional place to date?" When you experience a divorce, you may think the fix to healing is having another mate. You may be easily persuaded by others to date. You might even see your ex and they've already moved on with someone else, causing you to start questioning your worthiness or feel like you've been beaten to the punch line of being with someone. What this does to you emotionally is cloud your judgement to believe that you need someone in your life to prove not only to everyone else but also yourself that you can get someone too. This could result in you being in another relationship that doesn't serve you and is not in alignment with your values. When you walk away from a relationship chances are it wasn't able to provide what you needed. Step back and analyze what your needs are, what your morals are, who you are, how you communicate, and your love language so you can be in an emotionally healthy place. We live in such a busy world that we don't take the time to pause, get in a place of solitude and think. There's no time to evaluate and assess what happened in the past relationship and what's needed to live a thriving life. So many are in a rush to hop right back into the dating game only to end up with something similar to what they walked away from or something even worse.

What if I don't want anything serious?

When you're in a healed place and you want to date but don't desire anything serious, there's nothing wrong with casual dating. This doesn't mean to step outside of your values because you choose to casually date. Your values are for you to respect and protect yourself at all times because you don't want to jeopardize yourself, and be put in an emotional position to go backwards. I see some of the worst advice from some people. They say things like "Do what makes you feel good."or "You only live once." Those statements are true but avoid doing anything that can set you back. Feelings are not accurate at times and doing what makes you feel good now could cause a lot of hurt and pain for you later. This is why getting to know you matters. We can be easily influenced by the persuasion of others to the point that it compromises our own discernment. If you know that you could be unsure about things, seek some wise counsel to help gain a level of clarity. Your heart is precious and you must treat it as such.

If you are a person who desires to date with purpose where it involves something serious, that's okay as well. Understand that not everyone in this dating game is going to be like this. This is why healing matters because not only will you be prepared, you will always be aware of what you don't need to entertain.

If you don't want to date, then don't. It's that simple. You don't have anything to prove by dating if that's something you're not ready for.

Divorcing your story is to embrace your singleness and build that relationship up with you first because the relationship you have with yourself is a huge determining factor of the relationships you entertain.

Thrive it out!

What has been your view on being "single?" What are you going to do to embrace your singleness?

Tonya Carter

Chapter 17

Divorce the Weight

When I stepped on that scale and saw 239.2lbs, I asked myself the craziest question: How did this happen? How did I get here? Truth be told, I knew how I got there. I got here because of what I was eating. I had never been a small framed girl, but I never reached that high on the scale either. I had spiraled out of control. I was an emotional eater. I ate for every occasion. Happy, mad, sad or glad...I ate. I didn't even have to be really hungry, I ate because it was there. I decided to do something about it. Over the course of nine months, I lost a total of 80 pounds. People would ask "What did you do?" As if it what some form of a magic pill that I had that no one could get their hands on. There wasn't anything magical about it. It was just acknowledging that what I was eating wasn't working and I needed to start training myself to do the opposite to get different results. It was simple but not always easy. I was determined because I wasn't satisfied with my size and feeling sorry for myself wasn't going to change it. I was extremely proud of the accomplishment of losing the weight, but even though I looked good on the outside, I still wasn't healthy on the inside.

I had a lot of internal baggage. Even though I changed the way I ate and worked out to create healthy results on losing weight, it didn't change the way I felt about myself to attract healthy relationships in all areas of my life. Internally, I was addicted to pain and drama even though initally I didn't know I was. When I found myself entertaining some of the same types of people and having the same type of arguments, I thought that they were the problem and I wasn't. But, if that's what I not only attracted but entertained, wouldn't that mean that there was something going on inside of me?

There's a song by Erykah Badu called "Bag Lady". In the song it states:

Bag lady you gone hurt your back
Dragging all them bags like that
I guess nobody ever told you
All you must hold on to

Is you, is you, is you
One day all them bags gone get in your way
One day all them bags gone get in your way
I said one day all them bags gone get in your way
One Day all them bags gone get in your way

The song came out in the year of 2000. I didn't know what everything in the song meant at the time but as I became older and wiser and really listened to the lyrics, I realized that I was that bag lady. Here I am saying I wanted a new life, but I was taking the same type of weight with me. I wasn't unpacking and making my load lighter. I was still carrying the weight of not feeling worthy that all men are the same and I was not enough. The weight of believing that this is all I can get. The weight of believing that if you're a single mom, that no one would want you. I know it's simple to say, "I'm not going to deal with this same kind of treatment I dealt with before in my previous relationship" but if you have the weight of "I'm not worthy" traveling with you, then there's a high probability that you will repeat what you walked away from. Thriving requires developing healthy relationships but in order to create those relationships, we must establish an internal healthy relationship with ourselves.

When you have developed a culture of settling, you've established values of being mistreated, disrespected, verbally abused, and for many even physically abused. You want more but your past prohibits that due to the mental and emotional bags of settling and living in the past that are traveling with you. Experiencing these different things conditions your mindset of believing that this is true about you. If you meet someone and they're a great person, you don't want to ruin something that could be great for you just because of what happened in your previous relationship. You don't want to find yourself comparing someone else to what your ex may have done such as infidelity, lying, and/or keeping secrets. You don't want to believe that because you've encountered that situation with your ex that you're going to just automatically have this same experience with another individual. That's what you call baggage. You're believing that because you've experienced it, that you're going to encounter it over and over again. Therefore, you're not giving another relationship a fair chance because you're already going in with the mindset of believing that this is what's going to happen. Walking the journey of a new life requires you to drop off any weight that you're carrying that will not create the life you want to design. This new road traveled will require you to drop things off as well as pick things up. The lighter the load becomes the better the journey will be.

Drama Baggage

Do you carry bags of drama? Before you react, let me explain. Before I took this path, I didn't think I had bags of drama. I believed that he was the issue and everything around me was. This made me okay with being a victim. It also made me okay with how I responded to things. There were tons of arguments in our relationship and I found myself believing that had he changed then I wouldn't have to argue. I also found myself being an enabler by always rescuing him leaving me angry in the end because nothing had changed. Not only does that place blame, that also showed that I wanted a level of control that required me to stay the same and for him to change. The lack of responsibility was there and the focus on what he needed to do was there, causing me to not focus or take responsibility for myself. For a while, I didn't allow myself to see this. One reason was because I wasn't ready for this level of ownership and I was still stuck in my ideal story. Again, because I was this "good wife" that did everything from cooking, cleaning, working, making sure the bills were paid and taking care of the home, etc. I allowed all those qualities to cover this behavior. Does this make him innocent? ABSOLUTELY NOT! Remember, this isn't about him so it's important that you only make this about you. This is what could occur when you don't see the drama that you played:

1. You remain a victim and don't allow yourself to become a problem solver.

2. Anything outside of this behavior could be considered abnormal for you if this has been a long term pattern.

3. You will not establish healthy relationships due to unhealthy relationship drama patterns, causing any form of a relationship of any kind to fail.

4. You will continue to entertain this same type of relationship repeatedly.

You may not see this right away because it could be something that you're unconsciously doing. You may have never paid attention to or it might be due to your current emotional patterns but if the goal is to thrive, we must detach ourselves from what will never work. For some, our baggage could come from our upbringing where it had been considered normal, but in reality was a level of dysfunction. Drama comes in all kinds of forms and if we want healthy relationships we must identify the unhealthy drama patterns we've created. Reflect on these questions:

Are you a bag lady? What relationship bags are you holding on to that you need to drop off? What is your drama baggage? Do you find yourself making everything more than what it is? Do you overreact to receive an unhealthy level of attention? Do you constantly play the "woe is me" game? Do you go overboard doing for others only to leave yourself resentful in the end to make others feel sorry for you? Do you have an unhealthy level of control?

Divorcing your story requires you to divorce the baggage because it will get in the way of your present and your future. In the words of Erykah Badu, "Pack light."

Thrive it out!

Identify one unhealthy bag that you're carrying? How will this interfere with your vision? What is an actionable step to stay unpacking this bag?

Chapter 18

Divorce Isolation

Being "independent" is a great thing. I think it's great to be able to figure things out on your own and not solely depend on anyone for everything. There's strength in being independent but there's also a downside to being society's version of independent. There's this belief that because you're independent, that you never need anybody which is a false truth. No matter how independent you are, we are designed for community. We are designed for a village. There's a famous African proverb that states, "It takes a village to raise a child." This means that it takes an entire community of individuals to help children grow and become healthy. Even though I believe this to be true, it's also true that it takes a village to help us as adults to grow and become healthy as well.

Even though being independent is a great quality, it doesn't mean to do life alone. You don't want your divorce to put you in a mindset of being a standalone person because that's not the solution. I totally understand how easy it is to become a loner because of what you might have experienced in your marriage or just from the absence of others who you thought would have been there for you. Some have failed you. Many didn't do what they said they were going to do and now you put up this shield of protection. You begin blocking out the world, believing that because you've been disappointed by people who you loved and trusted, that the solution is to put a wall up or live by the motto of doing it by yourself. When you tune the entire world out, this is not a way to win. You're actually losing because you're blocking your potential blessings on who can be a help to you.

In 2012, a few years after my divorce, my ex decided to move out of state. It wasn't close either. It was actually on the opposite side of the United States. By this time, our children were only four and eight years old. That move impacted our children and as a parent it impacted me. I was laid off again which totaled up to five job losses in a four year timeframe. I though about how this would impact me as a parent. I often wondered how it would affect his relationship with our children? It's one thing to be divorced but what I didn't do was create children by myself. During that time, I would wonder if he factored everything into his decision or if it was just something he wanted to do for himself. As always I felt left to figure it out. Honestly, I thought this was a very selfish move. It was far and I felt like this was not fair to me as the mother of his children or his kids. This annoyed me so much and caused some level of isolation. It created thoughts of believing that everything was up to me to carry and figure out on my own. I've always considered myself to be a "figure outer." I've always been a person to just get it done but even with having that trait, it can become overwhelming in certain aspects of life.

For a long time, I had the "independent woman" syndrome. I felt the need to figure it all out and I didn't allow myself to be humble enough to ask for help. I never liked to ask for help because my philosophy was that asking others indicated that I wasn't capable. I was often disappointed by others, and I didn't want anyone to throw it back up in my face that they helped me, so I just shut everyone out and attempted to figure everything out. I didn't like to receive help when it was offered either. When people would offer I would reject it. I would always say "I'm good" which caused me to block many blessings. It's crazy because I would always help others but wouldn't allow myself to receive help. I really thought I could do and be all things. I was trying to be superwoman and supermom. I know it's often perceived as a badge of honor to be this woman but I beg to differ. As a mom, I thought I could do it all. I believed that I could stretch myself over capacity and still be my best self. I thought I could overcompensate and give my kids absolutely everything and it wouldn't do me any damage. That is false. When you experience something like a divorce, there's a level of guilt that you may have of believing that you've failed your children because you're no longer with the other parent. It could be that the other parent isn't as active as you would like for them to be. You might feel that you must fill that void by going over and beyond for your children. It could also be your ego that you have something to prove to either the other parent or yourself. You create this mindset that you're going to do it with or without them, even if it involves you exhausting yourself and going financially broke to do so.

Being this woman was killing me mentally, emotionally and financially. I started experiencing panic attacks and anxiety because I was overwhelmed from trying to do it all. We think we can handle it but your body will tell you otherwise. It was time to redefine what being superwoman and supermom meant. I could no longer attempt to figure everything out because I was exhausting myself. I had to get out of this place of isolation because if I wanted to thrive, I couldn't do it alone. I needed help and I had to welcome it with intention. I had to realize that just because people who I thought would help me didn't, that didn't mean no one else will. As a mom, I couldn't fill the void of the other parent. That wasn't my responsibility. No matter what I did, it wasn't going to erase the fact that their dad and I were no longer together. What I could do was be the best mother I could be. For this to happen, I had to release the mom guilt, the ego, and accept that the dynamics of our household had changed. Understanding this allowed me to start working on being a better woman which also crossed over into being a better mother.

You don't have to put yourself in a position to be so drained where you're not being good to yourself. Your children deserve the best version of you and this will not get you there. When you're your best self, you create healthy relationships and you teach your children how to have healthy relationships as well. The redefined version of superwoman knows that it's okay to take the cape off and ask for help. This doesn't make you less of a woman or mom, it makes you better because you know what you can handle.

Divorcing your story involves a village because you cannot travel this journey alone.

Thrive it out!

Ask yourself: Am I going into this isolation mode where I feel like I don't need anybody? What makes it hard to ask for help or accept it? Are I suffering with mom guilt because of what has taken place? What is one thing I can do to stop isolating myself and dismiss the mom guilt?

Chapter 19

Divorce Your Limitations

My father experienced a heart attack in March of 2015. When I received the phone call from my mom I just started crying. I love my dad. He's my superhero and the thought of not having him here frightened me. It's funny how life changes instantly. The day before this took place, he was at my house. The following day he was in the hospital. After I left visiting my dad that night, I came home and started thinking about my own life. At this time, it was close to five years since I'd been divorced and even though I had moved on from it emotionally, I realized that overall I just wasn't happy. Even though I finally had a stable job, the kids were doing well, and life was pretty okay, I knew in the back of my mind I wasn't satisfied or fulfilled in life.

My father's heart attack showed me that I wasn't pleased with the direction my life was going. I never really loved the career I was in and I just wanted more than what life was giving me. This experience allowed me to see things much clearer than before. My initial thought was that life was going to hand me what I wanted because I was a good person. I worked, I wasn't harming anyone, and I took care of my kids. This caused me to believe that I deserved it. It created a false sense of entitlement because of what I went through. I thought I should receive what was owed to me automatically, but that's not how it works. One of my biggest revelations was that life will hand you ANYTHING but it's up to you whether to accept or reject it. Life only gives you what you intentionally go after. That night when I was home thinking about my life, I came to the conclusion that I took whatever life handed to me. I allowed life to give me jobs with less pay that I never wanted. I allowed life to give me relationships that I never really wanted. I allowed life to determine how far I could go. Life was giving me all kinds of garbage but I was the one who believed this was all I could get. I felt like life wasn't fair and guess what? It isn't and it never will be. Life is never going to give you the best on its own. It's up to you to take the best by realizing that you can create your life by design rather than accepting it by default. I needed to know what else I was supposed to be doing with my life. That night I humbled myself, prayed and ask God "Why am I here?"

My dad's heart attack taught me two things. It taught me that I wasn't living the life that I wanted and no one is born to stay. It was time to get more serious about my life and stop going with the flow. Every day was the same type of day and I never liked it, I just became comfortable with it. I had to get transparent on about how I felt. There was a level of self-awareness that showed me that there were layers that I needed to peel back even further. At this point, this wasn't about the divorce, it was all about me and my life's direction. I just didn't feel like life had meaning. There I was with two beautiful kids, healthy, and able to pay the bills but still felt unfulfilled. I was grateful but something was missing. This was something that no one could fulfill. Not a relationship, a job, money or even my kids. It was something that was bigger than me. It was called purpose. At that time, I didn't know that's what it was. I never knew anything about purpose not to mention the realization that I even had one. No one told me that I had a gift and no one told me that I had meaning. My only definition for purpose in life was to work, pay bills, take care of the kids and possibly have some fun in between.

Figuring out why I was here was an inward job.

I had to start digging deeper into why I'm really here. One of the first books that helped me get more clarity was *"The Wealth Choice"* by Dennis Kimbro. It wasn't just about them becoming millionaires. What inspired me was the journey of getting to the success that they've accomplished. One of my favorite stories in the book was the one on Cathy Hughes, who is an entrepreneur, radio personality and business executive. Back in 1979, Cathy and her husband bought their own radio station. They finally found a lender after being rejected thirty two times. Shortly after her marriage ended and the radio station wasn't doing well. This forced her and her son to move out of their apartment and move into the station to make ends meet. Over time the station started turning a profit due to the success of her talk show. The station grew into a multimedia company with more than sixty stations across the globe, as well as a television network, TV One. Reading her story shows that the life you want to create can still happen even after those adversities that you thought would hold you back. Cathy chose to design her life. Even though I had no feelings towards my divorce anymore, I realized that I was still connected to a story of believing that being a divorced single mom meant I had to just accept whatever life had to offer. I developed a belief that I had lost control and had to settle but underneath that belief was a woman who desired more.

One thing I always loved to do was to talk, but it was never really considered a gift. Think about it. Whoever thought a person will have a gift of talking? However, that was my voice. That was the voice that I minimized because in my eyes it seemed more like a curse than a gift. Throughout my years growing up, I always stayed in trouble at school. I had N's and U's in conduct for talking all the time. My mom had to constantly come up to the school because I stayed in trouble for always talking. I even got a reward for being "Most Talkative" in high school. I just didn't know how to be quiet. I was always asked, "Why do you talk so much? Why don't you just be quiet?" When you hear that all the time, who would consider that being a gift? It made me believe that I had a problem and my talking was an issue therefore it made me beleive that it wasn't useful.

I was always the "go to" person for many people especially people who had experienced a breakup. People always came to me for advice but I didn't think nothing of it until my dad experienced the heart attack. I was often asked why am I not speaking or coaching but I would always brush it off by using kids, bills, and being a single mom as the excuse, knowing deeply inside that this was something that I had a passion for. I always minimized my gift because in my eyes I thought "Who am I to help people?"or "Who would want to hear me speak? Who would want to hear what I have to say?" I finally stopped resisting, got out of my own way and decided to take that leap of faith. I learned to believe that my voice was my gift. My father's heart attack made me see that I don't have all the time in the world and I want the life that was meant for me. My purpose was always there but it was up to me to welcome it in with open arms and embrace it. We minimize our purpose or we deny our purpose because of what we've experienced. We let what others say about us hinder our ability to shine therefore dimming our light. I want you to let your light shine.

Back in 2016, I had lunch with my mentor. By this time I had an understanding on what I wanted to do. I was on the journey of personal development for over a year and it brought so much clarity. He asked me "What do you fear?" and my response was that I feared failing but I also feared being highly successful. I know that may sound impossible but it was true. It was like I established a life of being mediocre even though I hated that place. I was in bondage of being average and had difficulty believing that I could have and become more. I limited myself based on what I saw around me and what I've experienced but I couldn't stop thinking about my purpose. It stayed on my heart and my mind all the time. I knew that this was something special but making the decision to take the leap was one of the toughest but most rewarding decisions I've made. So much has happened within me by doing this. This wasn't just about what I'm doing, it's the woman I was becoming in the process. My purpose unleashed something in me that I don't think would've ever transpired had I not taken that leap. I've redefined, reinvented and redeveloped into who I was always supposed to be. If someone told me ten years ago that I would be doing this, I wouldn't have believe them because of the limits I had placed on myself. As I look back, I thought my experiences were my punishment, but it was preparation for who I am now and who I'm going to be later. We often compartmentalize our lives but to be whole is to understand that we can thrive in all areas of life. We often believe that our experiences limits us but they should unleash us to become limitless.

Divorcing your story is to stop placing periods where only commas should be.

I'm not sure on what my purpose is....

You may be unaware of what your purpose or passion is right now and that's okay. This took some time for me too. As you continue to heal things will become clearer on what your direction should be in life. Below are a few questions to help you.

1. What are some things you love to do? (These are

things that come easy for you.)

2. What are some of your key strengths that you minimize? Knowing your strengths is essential. Visit https://www.tonyacarter.com to schedule a consultation on "Unleashing Your Inner Queen."

3. According to your vision statement from Chapter One, does it bring a level of passion to you? If it doesn't then go back and revise.

4. Ask some people you trust. Sometimes we're unable to see what others see in us. Don't dismiss what they're saying. Take it as useful information to help you.

Thrive it out!

Ask yourself: What am I hiding? What am I minimizing about myself that I know I should be doing but have allowed the adversity of life to get in the way? What have people told me that I'm not capable of doing but I know in my heart that I can't escape it because it brings me joy and fulfillment?

Chapter 20

Marry a New Game Plan

Earlier, I mentioned that the most common thing I hear from women who experienced a divorce is that they've lost themselves, when chances are they may have never known who they were to begin with. When you become so consumed with being a wife and a mom, you believe that should be your entire world when it shouldn't. It's extremely important to have your own life. I believe this is one of many reasons why moving forward is challenging. Maybe you gave up so much for the relationship where it left you depleted. You may have believed that in order for your relationship to be successful that you needed to shrink yourself for it to work. For some, they were extremely codependent on their spouses, causing them to not have anything else outside of the relationship. Whatever the reason, that's changing now.

To become whole and well, we must focus on the different areas that developing wholeness requires and you will need a guide for making it happen. Living life by design involves a blueprint. You don't want to just read the book, put it up and live life like you did before. You will not get to your vision that way. This has to be intentional today, tomorrow and forever. To move forward, you have to know what you're moving towards and for that to happen you must set goals. Thinking about them, verbalizing them and saying you want to do better simply isn't enough. It's important that you be clear and specific on the goals you want to achieve. According to an article in Psychology Today, goal setters see future possibilities and the bigger picture. The act of setting goals is also connected with self-confidence, motivation and independence. Studies also show that people who wrote down their goals were 33% more successful in achieving them than those who only kept a mental note of them.

Developing wholeness involves different areas of your life. Below are different areas that your life should consist of:

1. **Faith** – Your belief system.
2. **Personal Development** -- Your mental and emotional state of being.

3. **Health** – Are you resting, eating foods that your body responds to well and exercising?

4. **Family/Relationships** - Your relationships with your kids, parents, friends, and/or romantic relationships?

5. **Occupational** – Satisfaction in your career.

6. **Finances** – Financial Freedom, Generational Wealth.

7. **Social Life/Recreation** – Your leisure time.

If you have another area that's important to you then feel free to add it.

Below is how to start setting small clear goals.

1. **Analyze your areas of importance** - On a scale of 1-10 with 10 being the highest, analyze how you're doing in the areas listed.

2. **Rate those areas** - Next, choose 1-3 areas that you can start improving on.

3. **Let's get clarity** - Now it's time to get VERY clear and specific on the goals in those areas you've chosen to start with. Many are too vague when

setting goals but the more specific you are, the more the aim you have. Don't be afraid to be detailed about what it is you want. For instance, don't say you want to make more money. Set a specific amount of what you want to make!

A useful tip when setting a clear goal is to have a "why", "how" and "what" – What is the reason behind this goal? How strong is that reason? For example, if your goal is to pay off $25K of debt, why is this important? The stronger the why in getting this done, the more motivated you'll be in accomplishing the goal. Because you know this will create financial freedom and that will be your driving force to get it done.

4. **Stay on track** - How will the goal be tracked and measured? If the goal is to pay $25K off in two years then how often will progress be tracked? Weekly, Monthly, Quarterly? It's important to set dates to stay on track.

5. **Is this realistic right now?** - Can this be achievable and is this relevant right now? For every season, there are goals that are achievable and some that aren't. This isn't implying what you want could never happen but you want to make sure that the goal that's being set matches with where you are. It's important that the goal still challenges you,

but it needs to be realistic and necessary during this particular time. Maybe paying off 25K in two years may not be achievable right now because you could be just getting back on your feet. You don't want to discourage yourself by setting a goal too high where it may not be achievable. Maybe it should be three years but it's essential to be realistic with where you are to set an attainable goal.

6. **Let's put a time stamp on it** – If the realistic goal is to pay off 25K of debt in 36 months, how can this happen? How can you simplify this to hit the mark in 36 months?

   a. This means that you will need to pay off around $8,333.33 yearly
   b. This is around $694.44 monthly
   c. Which is $160.25 weekly
   d. Which equals to roughly around $22.83 daily

7. **Accountability** – Get around some people whogoing to hold you accountable. You cannot elevate in an environment that's stagnant. Sure you may be motivated now but what about the days when you're not as motivated? That's where

the discipline counts the most. I wish I could tell you EVERYDAY I'm pumped, but not always. There are days when I am tired, which is why I had to change my circle to keep going. When I started being around different people with different mindsets, I moved differently. It's okay to outgrow your environment. You're not a sellout because you desire more but you're selling out by staying somewhere you no longer belong.

8. **Celebrate along the way** – I encourage you to celebrate every small win along the way. When you look at the goal you're trying to accomplish, it can seem far away where you don't think you're making progress but every small step is a step. All these small steps is what will create the biggest impact. It's important to be your own cheerleader along this journey.

9. **Make adjustments when needed** – Things happen so don't give up, just make the adjustments. If three years is too short then let's readjust the goal. Let's simplify it even more but whatever you do, **DO NOT STOP!**

10. Repeat – The journey to thriving has no destination. Repeat steps 1-9, and before you know it you will have a lot of things accomplished,

then it just becomes your new normal.

Divorcing your story is recognizing that the new life you want is a marathon and not a sprint. By setting goals, being intentional and executing, this will create a compound effect of change and you will see the results of your work.

Thrive it out!

List 1-3 areas that you would like to start working on and one goal for each of those areas. Using the steps listed above, how can you make this goal an accomplishment? How can you make it attainable?

Epilogue

You've reached the end of this book but this isn't the end of your story. Take a moment to reflect. Where are you emotionally right now? Where are you mentally? Do you feel like you're a little or a lot better? Wherever you are, be proud of yourself and DO NOT STOP! We can't simply stop something when it's not happening as fast as we would like it to, or believe that once we've read or completed something, that there's no more work. I had this illusion myself. I believed that because I made the decision to live a thriving life that everything was going to happen immediately, but that's not how living a thriving life works.

Society is now an instant gratification world.

With social media being the hub for people to show the highlights of their "best" lives, you can often find yourself in the comparison trap comparing your life to others. This creates a misconception that everyone is living this great life that you're missing out on. With the download of apps on your phone, all it takes is one click of a button and you're able to get what you want whether that be placing an order or buying something new. But creating a new life takes more than pics on social media and one click access. It's work. It's commitment.

Should you be fully healed by now? Everyone is different when it comes to healing. Your emotional wounds could be deep to the point where it takes not only time but action to heal. Healing isn't an overnight process so I don't want you to stop. For some they stop because the progress isn't as fast as they want it to be OR they don't "feel" like it, but thriving is recognizing that it's going to take patience. Don't you owe that to yourself? Aren't you worth the effort? Even though you've finished all twenty chapters of this book, tomorrow should be chapter twenty one for you, the next day chapter twenty two and so on. What would those chapters say? Every day when you wake up how will you choose to live out your day? Will it be purposeful or purposeless? Will you decide to heal or stay in hurt? This is what divorcing your story looks like. It's about understanding that you have the choice to decide how you want to live. Every single day from this point is still a day of healing and personal growth. As long as you have breath in your body, there is never a final destination to thriving. There's always some area in your life where you can grow and become better, but in order to do that, you have to divorce stopping.

Make a declaration today that you're going to keep going no matter what. No matter how you feel and no matter how uncertain the road ahead is. Reflect on where you were on chapter one versus where you are now. What has improved? What progress has been made? What is the one thing that you do see a lot clearer than you did before? If it's just one thing that means something has changed in your life. Just think about what will happen if you kept going and how much more will change. In other words, keep doing what's working! This is what builds resilience and a better version of yourself.

What are you going to do to keep going? What are you going to do every day to get to the vision you wrote down? Are there certain chapters in the book that you need to go back to and reflect on? If so, please do so and do it as many times as you need to. Set a small goal, accomplish it and set another one. This is what constantly creates wins and the momentum for you to stay in the game.

Be proud of yourself and take a moment to write down everything you've learned and what has gotten better. Tell someone how this has helped you and please email me at info@divorceyourstorybook.com and tell me what has changed in your life after reading this book.

Resources

Helen Keller. (n.d.). Retrieved from https://www.biography.com/activist/helen-keller

25 Maya Angelou Quotes to Inspire Your Life. (2019, May 21). Retrieved from https://www.goalcast.com/2017/04/03/maya-angelou-quotes-to-inspire-your-life/

Brown, B. (2010). The Gifts of Imperfection: Let Go of Who You Think You're Supposed to Be and Embrace Who You Are. Hazelden Publishing.

Brown, B. (2015). Daring Greatly: How the Courage to be Vulnerable Transforms the Way We Live, Love, Parent, and Lead. London, England: Penguin.

Definition of BLAME. (n.d.). Retrieved from https://www.merriam-webster.com/dictionary/blame

Definition of OWNERSHIP. (n.d.). Retrieved from https://www.merriam-webster.com/dictionary/ownership

Emotional Coping and Divorce. (n.d.). Retrieved from https://www.mentalhelp.net/articles/emotional-coping-and-divorce/

Five Stages Of Grief - Understanding the Kubler-Ross Model. (2019, April 11). Retrieved from https://www.psycom.net/depression.central.grief.html

Goal-Setting Is Linked to Higher Achievement. (n.d.). Retrieved from https://www.psychologytoday.com/us/blog/the-moment-youth/201803/goal-setting-is-linked-higher-achievement

Dictionary by Merriam-Webster: America's most-trusted online dictionary. (n.d.). Retrieved from https://www.merriam-webster.com/

Dweck, C. S. (2006). *Mindset: The New Psychology of Success.* New York, NY: Random House.

Editors, H. (2019, April 4). Maya Angelou is born. Retrieved from https://www.history.com/this-day-in-history/maya-angelou-is-born

Emotional Coping and Divorce. (n.d.). Retrieved from https://www.mentalhelp.net/articles/emotional-coping-and-divorce/

The Essential Guide to Writing S.M.A.R.T. Goals. (2019, May 16). Retrieved from https://www.smartsheet.com/blog/essential-guide-writing-smart-goals

Forgiveness: Your Health Depends on It. (n.d.).

Retrieved from https://www.hopkinsmedicine.org/health/wellness-and-prevention/forgiveness-your-health-depends-on-it

Maya Angelou Biography. (n.d.). Retrieved from https://www.notablebiographies.com/An-Ba/Angelou-Maya.html

Munroe, M. (2005). *Single, Married, Separated and Life after Divorce.* Shippensburg, PA: Destiny Image Publishers.

Phenomenal Woman by Maya Angelou. (n.d.). Retrieved from https://www.poetryfoundation.org/poems/48985/phenomenal-woman

Roberta Hoskie. (n.d.). Retrieved from https://www.robertahoskie.net/

Your Ex After Divorce ? How To Establish Boundaries. (n.d.). Retrieved from https://www.womansdivorce.com/ex-after-divorce.html

About the Author

Tonya S. Carter, born in Atlanta and raised in Decatur. She decided to devote her life helping women to divorce their stories of hurt, pain, and past experiences that keeps them captive from living exceptional & thriving lives. She's a graduate of DeVry University where she obtained her Bachelors of Science in Information Technology as well as Central Michigan University where she received her Master's in Information Resource Management. Although her education afforded her a career to provide for her family, this wasn't the work that Tonya was called to do. She was called to heal women and help them through times where they felt defeated, lost and uncertain of the future. Her mission is to help women shift from feeling defeated to experiencing victory. From feeling lost to being found by unleashing their inner Queen. From uncertainty to building faith so that they're able to live the life that is destined for them. One of the sayings she lives by is "Control what you can, release what you cannot." Once we understand that the only person we have full control over is ourselves, then life becomes simple.

To connect with Tonya for coaching, speaking or to follow on social media

Instagram - @mstonyaspeaks

Facebook – MsTonya Speaks

LinkedIn – Tonya Carter

Website: www.tonyacarter.com

Divorce Coaching: www.divorceyourstory.com

Email: info@tonyacarter.com

Do you need assistance? Do you need a coach to help you get further than where you are? If you feel like you need more and you want to work with me then visit my website at www.divorceyourstory.com or email: info@ divorceyourstory.com.

Printed in Great Britain
by Amazon

67679240R00113